PLANTS & GARDENS

BROOKLYN BOTANIC GARDEN RECORD

The Natural Lawn
& Alternatives

First printing, 1993
Second printing, 1995

Plants & Gardens, Brooklyn Botanic Garden Record (ISSN 0362-5850)

is published quarterly at 1000 Washington Ave., Brooklyn, N.Y. 11225, by the **Brooklyn Botanic Garden, Inc.**

Subscription included in Botanic Garden membership dues ($35.00 per year).

ISBN # 0-945352-80-8

Brooklyn Botanic Garden

STAFF FOR THIS EDITION:

MARGARET ROACH, GUEST EDITOR

JANET MARINELLI, EDITOR

BARBARA B. PESCH, DIRECTOR OF PUBLICATIONS

AND THE EDITORIAL COMMITTEE OF THE BROOKLYN BOTANIC GARDEN

BEKKA LINDSTROM, ART DIRECTOR

JUDITH D. ZUK, PRESIDENT, BROOKLYN BOTANIC GARDEN

ELIZABETH SCHOLTZ, DIRECTOR EMERITUS, BROOKLYN BOTANIC GARDEN

STEPHEN K-M. TIM, VICE PRESIDENT, SCIENCE & PUBLICATIONS

FRONT AND BACK COVER: PHOTOGRAPH BY KEN DRUSE

PLANTS & GARDENS
BROOKLYN BOTANIC GARDEN RECORD

The Natural Lawn

& ALTERNATIVES

VOL. 49, NO. 3, AUTUMN 1993

HANDBOOK #136

Introduction	by Margaret Roach	4
The Purposeful Lawn	by John Trexler	8
Fields and Meadows	by John Trexler	12
A Case for the Chemical-Free Lawn	by Warren Schultz	18
Eight Steps to a Pesticide-Free Lawn	by Warren Schultz	24
Turf Tips		28
Grasses for Every Region		28
Grass Zones of the United States		29
The Lazy Gardener's Guide to Fertilizing Lawn		30
How Low Should You Mow?		31
Building Better Grass Seeds	by Marie Pompei	32
How to Renovate Your Lawn	by Maria Cinque	38
Buffalograss Lawns	by Sally Wasowski with Andy Wasowski	44
The Lawnless Landscape	by Sally Wasowski with Andy Wasowski	50
Moss Lawns	by David Benner	60
Ground Covers for Shade	by Ken Druse	68
Sedge Lawns	by John Greenlee	75
Prairie	by Neil Diboll	81
Index		93

Introduction

||||||||||||||||||||||||||||||||||||||||

We get red in the face pushing the mower around week after week, determined to keep the green, green grass of home in check. Instead of treating it like the rest of our landscape plants and encouraging flowers, fruit and seeds to be set, we thwart its sex drive again and again with our noisy, violent rounds.

Between beheadings, though, we water the grass like crazy and, several liberally applied times a season, force-feed the lawn, urging the same blades we crewcut into submission to grow, grow, grow.

What's wrong with this picture? Plenty, I think, starting with our schizoid dilemma: do we want the grass to grow, or do we want to make it stop?

America's love affair with the lawn borders on a fatal attraction — though it needn't be that way, as this handbook proposes and I hope proves. Under the guise of beautifying the postwar suburban sprawl that we built in the name of progress, we fell too deeply in love to think clearly. And it goes way beyond the grow/don't grow conundrum.

The Environmental Protection Agency estimates that 70 million pounds of active pesticide ingredient (the vast part of each bag you buy, the filler, isn't even counted in that total) is used each year by Americans to treat their 40 million acres of precious turf. In pursuit of what amounts to a living Astroturf — unreasonably perfect in every way, please, without a weed or blemish — we spend $6.9 billion a year (1991 figures) on do-it-yourself products alone, says the nonprofit National Gardening Association in Vermont. And we spend lots more hiring professionals to do the work for us, too.

A hard change is gonna come, and in fact is already under way in many corners of this nation, and it is being staged by gardeners like the ones represented in this volume. This handbook celebrates the start of the lawncare revolution, offering tips on how to care for your traditional lawn in a safer way, and alternatives for various regions of the country should you be among those ready to unshackle yourself from the mower at last, and try planting something besides grass.

Chemical-free lawncare is being touted as being to the 90s what recycling was to the 80s — the thing to do, the savvy way to handle things. Exciting developments like safer remedies for problems and grass breeds that grow slower, greener and healthier naturally, are making a "green" — as in environmental — lawn possible.

Around the country, forward-thinking communities are testing bans on lawncare's worst aspects: forbidding loud, gas-guzzling mowers; outlawing pesticides and herbicides or requiring those who use them to post prominent signs that say so; severely limiting watering, and, in the most dramatic cases of all, making the

installation of a traditional lawn against the law altogether.

Of course, there's nothing so soft underfoot, or so nice to lie on, as a well tended lawn. On beautiful summer days, I wouldn't trade mine in for anything — even the smell of fresh-cut grass pleases me, filed as it is into my deepest memory since as far back as my first summer, I suppose.

But my lawn is smaller than it once was, and shrinking every season, in favor of groundcovers, flower and shrub gardens, and even a patch of meadow. I haven't fed it or limed it in eight years. I've also given up my images of perfection, and learned to live with some weeds. Five to ten percent weeds doesn't warrant chemical warfare, the new thinking goes, so I just mow them and enjoy their fresh green color in the crazy quilt that is my lawn. When I get up from my nap on this pleasing outdoor carpet — clover, crabgrass and all — I'll dig out a few dandelions in the name of a beautiful, but chemical-free, future.

— *Margaret Roach*

MARGARET ROACH *is the garden editor of* Newsday *and* New York Newsday *and a long-time organic gardener.*

7

The Purposeful Lawn

Life is too short to be spending purposeless moments mowing your lawn

BY JOHN TREXLER

I've had half a lifetime to think about lawns and their place in the home landscape. During this time I've developed both a love of a good lawn and a common-sense philosophy about its role in the home landscape: lawns are expensive both in dollars and in the time it takes to maintain them. If a lawn does not have a well defined function, it should be permitted to be field or revert back to forest. Life is too short to be spending purposeless moments mowing the lawn.

My earliest memory of lawn is not pleasurable, but rather one of the unending maintenance they entail. One Saturday morning thirty-plus years ago I sat on the grass with my father, asparagus knife in hand, carefully extracting dandelions and plantain, being careful not to leave a trace of root.

"Why is this important?" I asked my father.

"Because," was his only reply.

My suburban upbringing introduced me to thousands of lawns. They were pretty, and I regarded them without prejudice. There was one lawn that I still remember with awe: Dr. Wheeler's in Coronado, California. I was the only child permitted into his paradise. It was perfect, one hundred percent bent grass — beautiful, but now considered ecologically unsuitable for anything except perhaps a golf course. I would stand at the edge of this green carpet and stare at the lush garden beyond.

However, my early experiences with wielding an asparagus knife must have left an indelible impression. After high school I pursued an undergraduate degree in ornamental horticulture and heard countless times that "turf care" was a potentially profitable career. I chose to work in public horticulture instead.

Left: In the author's garden every patch of lawn has a purpose. Here it serves as a pathway between borders and beds.

After graduating I worked at Skylands, one of the grander examples of the golden age of American residential landscape design. While there I had the privilege of working with an old Scottish head gardener who filled my head with talk of the good old days, when caring for the 100-plus acres of lawn entailed dozens of workers crawling backwards, following a string and removing all weeds three feet on either side, then moving the string and repeating the action until all weeds were gone and the lawn was perfect. The lawns were also sponged every morning to remove dew, then powdered with fungicide to prevent disease. All for the sake of flawless lawn, lawn that served no practical function. I must admit I found this oddly romantic.

Common sense should help guide us as we develop and maintain our home landscapes. First and foremost, we need to understand that when we have acquired a home with land on which we can garden, that garden should give us pleasure — not worry, not resentment, but pleasure.

Using my own home garden in Boylston, Massachusetts, as an example, I will explain what I mean by a purposeful lawn. My small house and barn sit in the middle of a one-acre property. The driveway sits three feet south of the house, dividing the rectangular acre neatly in two. The half acre south of the driveway is half wooded and half unmowed lawn. The lawn had been mowed for many decades. I moved to the property just as the mowing season had ended, so I had the dormant season to think about the purpose of this lawn. The decision was easy, as the lawn's slope was too steep to be a useful recreational space, and too shady to be cultivated as a vegetable garden. So I decided to let it be field, with a mowed perimeter for neatness and access. The east side of the field, which borders the street, has become a screen of assorted deciduous and evergreen shrubs. This gives me privacy and spares any passersby who believe in the inviolability of manicured lawn the discomfort of witnessing this "radical" transformation.

The remaining half of my property, to the north of the house and barn, was level mowed lawn with a couple of unrelated island beds planted with assorted perennials and roses. This half acre gave me a canvas on which to create my garden. For the last five years I have methodically arranged a series of shrub and perennial borders on axes that can be viewed from various spots inside the house. The remaining grass serves as pathway through the borders and as open space for garden parties and passive lawn sports. I would guess that of the two thirds of an acre of lawn that I acquired, a sixth of an acre remains, all of which has purpose and gives pleasure.

My approach to lawn maintenance is simple. I mow it as often as necessary to maintain a consistently neat appearance. In my mind, if the lawn looks shaggy the

The amount of lawn on the property was reduced by 75 percent. Fields and flowerbeds replaced manicured turf.

whole garden looks bad. I cut the lawn to a length of three and a half to four inches. I have discovered that cutting the grass at a higher setting helps prevent weeds from getting established and conserves soil moisture during drought by shading the soil and base of the grass plant. When mowing, I catch the clippings in a bag and use them as mulch in the shrub borders. I fertilize the lawn with an organic base 10-10-10 fertilizer once every three years. I lime it with a granular limestone once every three years. I do not use herbicides. I am sometimes tempted to use a pre-emergent herbicide to prevent crabgrass from germinating. But I always forget, so every year crabgrass is part of my collection of "lawn plants."

I must conclude by saying that I really do like lawn. It is by far the simplest groundcover to maintain (as long as you have a relaxed approach). Lawn is for walking on and for playing and entertaining on. It is one of the most pragmatic elements of a garden. We just have to keep reminding ourselves of its useful function and the pleasure it should deliver.

JOHN TREXLER *is Director of the Tower Hill Botanic Garden in Boylston, Massachusetts.*

Fields and Meadows

*T*o my thinking, fields and meadows are the most dynamic of garden habitats. They pulse with life in a way that no other garden style can. They stimulate the senses in a hundred different ways and at the same time are very relaxing because they require such simple care.

A meadow is usually defined as a grass-dominated plant community that occurs naturally in the East (as opposed to prairie, which is native to the Midwest and Great Plains states). At Tower Hill Botanic Garden in Boylston, Massachusetts, where I am director, we distinguish between fields, or open areas of herbaceous plants where the soil is basically dry, and meadows, where the soil is moister.

My lawn philosophy can be seen on a larger scale here at Tower Hill. When

Left: Daffodils bloom in the fields at Tower Hill Botanic Garden in spring.
Above: An aerial view of the Garden.

Above: A mowed path will allow you to explore your meadow garden.

Right: One of the more formal mowed lawn areas at Tower Hill Botanic Garden.

the Worcester County Horticultural Society bought Tower Hill Farm seven years ago there were approximately 30 acres of open field and 100 acres of woodland. According to the garden's master plan, 95 acres, comprising over 20 individual gardens, will be developed. Only 3-1/2 of these 95 acres will be mowed lawn. Approximately 20 acres will be field and meadow.

Our fields and meadows are managed in the simplest way imaginable. We mow these spaces once a year after a killing frost, usually in November. We occasionally have to spot-mow certain areas during the growing season.

Because one of the benefits of field and meadow is that they attract field-nesting birds, it is important to identify and not disturb them when they are nesting. We are sometimes asked why we don't hay our fields in July. Two reasons: we

The meadow garden, above left, features butterfly weed, black-eyed Susan and phlox. Center: For a more restful effect, create a meadow of mostly grasses.

don't want to disturb the nesting birds, and we don't want to disturb the natural ripening process of the seeds of early-blooming plant species. We do not seed our fields and meadows with any canned product. We let nature take its course. This has been remarkably successful. We have an extraordinary selection of species that, with a few exceptions, appeared on their own. We have introduced bulbs of Canada lily (*Lilium canadensis*), seed of fringed gentian (*Gentianopsis crinita*) and daffodil bulbs to one of the drier slopes.

Our biggest problem is poison ivy. Before we owned Tower Hill, the fields were left unmowed for a few years. During this period, birds seeded poison ivy through-

PAMELA HARPER

Meadows provide a succession of bloom from spring until fall. Above right: Asters and goldenrods add bold splashes of color to a meadow in autumn.

out the 30 acres. We tried controlling it by mowing biweekly, starting in August. This did not seem to work. So now, starting in June, we spot spray the larger patches with Roundup, a systemic herbicide. This is proving to be successful.

Access through the fields is via one and a half miles of mowed path. The eight-foot-wide paths expose the visitor to the delights of these habitats. Benches along the paths encourage visitors to rest and enjoy the beauty.

If you have the space on your own property, savor the pleasures of field and meadow — don't force them into submission as lawns.

— *John Trexler*

A Case for the Chemical-Free Lawn

Lawn need not be an environmental villain. Here's how to kick the chemical habit

BY WARREN SCHULTZ

*T*he front lawn is under attack across America. It has become political-ly correct to bash this uniquely American institution. From the way some people talk, you'd think that those leaves of grass were respon-sible for the downfall of the environment, the poisoning of our water supply, the ill health of our populace, dwindling reservoirs and probably the recession, too.

Okay, so lawns don't produce bushels of vegetables and aren't the most biodi-verse horticultural creations. We can attend to such things in our backyards. After all, the front lawn has been called America's great contribution to world garden design, with all those patches of unfenced grass uniting us as a democracy and as a people.

Used judiciously, lawn need not be an environmental villain. We've been hearing a lot about the value of trees for their ability to convert carbon dioxide to oxygen and so lessen the greenhouse effect. Well, every tiny grass plant does the same thing. Multiply the 30,000,000 grass plants that make up an acre of lawn by the 30,000,000 acres of lawn in America and you've got a lot of oxygen.

One of the main complaints against lawns is that they are water hogs. Not true. There's precious little evidence to show that turf uses more water than trees and shrubs. In fact, studies have shown that a six-foot-tall tree has three times the evapotranspiration rate (and therefore uses three times the water) of Bermudagrass growing beneath its canopy.

That's not to say that lawns can't be major offenders, sucking up too much water, fertilizer, herbicide, insecticide and fungicide. But home lawns can pros-per without water and chemical indulgence. It's not lawns per se that are at fault. It's what we put on them.

The average American lawn is treated with five to ten pounds of pesticide per acre. And most of those chemicals are not the kind of thing you want blowing in the wind or flavoring your water.

About 40 different pesticides are commonly used on home lawns. Twelve of them are suspected human cancer causers. Twenty-one have been shown to cause long-term health effects in lab animals or humans, including birth defects, mutations or nervous system damage.

There's no question that pesticides we put on our lawns wind up elsewhere. In the recent U.S. Environmental Protection Agency groundwater survey, Dacthal, most frequently used on lawns, was the most commonly detected pesticide in water wells. And even suburban community wells were heavily contaminated with nitrates from fertilizers. (The intake of nitrates has been linked to cancer and "blue baby syndrome.")

That's the bad news. The good news is that you don't need that stuff on your lawn. Chemicals are just short-sighted responses to problems caused by trying to grow the wrong grass in the wrong place with the wrong techniques. In fact, in some ways chemicals make it more difficult to grow a lawn. They kill off beneficial organisms in the soil that normally would keep disease organisms in check. They wipe out beneficial insects that would control harmful ones. They weaken the grass plants by causing them to grow too fast and lush. And they do absolutely nothing to solve the cause of weed problems.

So how do you grow a lawn without chemicals?

Grow the Right Grass

It all starts with the grass. Most turf problems are caused by trying to grow the wrong grass in the wrong place. But now we have more options than ever. There's been an explosion of new turfgrass cultivars over the past ten years that make getting your lawn in order an easy prospect.

If you face a problem, there's probably now a grass that can handle it. Too little rain; too much heat? Tall fescue's fast- and deep-growing roots enable it to withstand heat and drought better than all other northern grasses. Too much shade? Fine fescues thrive in relatively shady conditions. Insects bugging your patch of turf? One of the biggest breakthroughs in recent turf breeding has been the development of insect-resistant perennial ryegrasses. See page 28 for recommended grasses for your region.

Though insect resistance is a new advance in turf varieties, disease resistance is not. The disease war is pretty much over, and the grasses have won. From brown patch to fusarium to dollar spot to powdery mildew, there are new turfgrass varieties for nearly any disease you can name. The new Kentucky bluegrasses and perennial ryes offer the best package of disease resistance.

You can have a lush lawn without resorting to chemical warfare. This lawn at Colonial Williamsburg is grown organically.

Use Natural Fertilizer

Sowing the right grass will get you off to a good start, but, of course, there's more to it than that. You have to work to overcome the chemical-quick-fix mentality. Start with fertilizer. Chemical lawn fertilizers are almost always full of high-analysis, water-soluble nitrogen. They are a here-today, gone-tomorrow proposition; constant reapplication is required because they have no residual action.

The grass will be stronger and more vigorous if it's fed slowly and steadily through the season with a natural fertilizer. Most natural forms of nitrogen are water insoluble. They stick around in the ground for a long time and soil acids and microorganisms slowly convert them to forms that plants can use.

There are plenty of natural sources of nitrogen: cow manure, bloodmeal, cottonseed meal, fish emulsion, leather tankage and mixed organic fertilizers. Dried poultry manure is probably the best option. One 25-pound bag of dried poultry manure will feed 1,000 square feet of lawn per year.

Don't Scalp Your Lawn

If you use natural fertilizers, your lawn doesn't grow out of control. And the lawn mower becomes a turf-management tool. Mowing is maybe the most important thing you will ever do to your lawn. Properly done, mowing can kill weeds, cure diseases, save water and provide fertilizer. By mowing high, you'll reduce stress on the grass and enable it to compete better with weeds. You'll also let the grass shade the soil to inhibit germination and growth of weeds.

Kentucky bluegrass will grow best if you cut it to three inches during the summer. Perennial ryegrass and fine fescues should be mowed a little bit shorter, 2-1/2 inches maximum, while tall fescues can be allowed to grow to four inches.

One remarkable study at the University of Rhode Island showed that high mowing alone could reduce crabgrass to virtually nothing. Left to its own devices in an unfertilized turf plot, crabgrass cover increased from year to year, reaching a high of 54 percent in the third year and dropping to 33 percent in the fifth year. But in a second plot the crabgrass cover steadily decreased from a high of 30 percent in the first year to seven percent in the fifth year. There was only one difference in the two plots: the first was mowed regularly at 1-1/4 inches, and the second was mowed regularly at 2-1/4 inches.

Invest in a Weed Popper

In general, the best defense against weeds is a healthy lawn. Thick and vigorous turf just doesn't allow much room for weeds. Of course you may have to step in from time to time to eradicate stubborn weeds. Herbicides may kill off those weeds, but they don't do anything to correct the problem. Unless those conditions — compacted soil, improper watering and mowing — are changed, the weeds will return, requiring more and more herbicides.

But you can rid a lawn of weeds without chemicals, and you don't have to spend a lot of time on your hands and knees doing it. There are several long-handled tools, weed poppers and pullers, that allow you to pull out persistent weeds, taproot and all, without much effort.

Yes, dandelions are particularly persistent. Their long taproots are hard to pull, and root pieces left behind will regenerate into new weeds. It's important to get to them when they're at their weakest — when they're blooming, and when food reserves in the roots are at their lowest. Dig out four to five inches of the root and chances are that any remaining root pieces won't have enough strength to send up another stalk.

Know Thine Insects

Natural insect control is even easier. The first step in natural lawn insect control is learning not to overreact. Get to know the enemies so that you know both what they look like and when to expect them.

There are natural controls, both biological and physical, that wipe out every turf pest. Sabadilla dust, for example, will control chinch bugs. (So will endophyte-enhanced grass varieties; see "Building Better Grasses.") Rotenone or diatomaceous earth will take care of billbugs. And insecticidal soap or Bt will control sod webworms. Milky spore is a good long-term control measure against Japanese beetle grubs, but it takes a few years to take effect.

Topdress to Keep Down Diseases

As for diseases, they're rarely a problem with the chemical-free lawn. The soil itself can keep problems in check. In healthy soil, disease pathogens are vastly outnumbered by non-pathogenic microfauna (amoebae, nematodes and insects) and microflora (bacteria, actinomycetes and fungi). They usually have the upper hand, and keep the disease-causing organisms in check unless outside intervention, such as a fungicide or herbicide application, upsets the equilibrium.

Applications of manure can increase the disease-fighting actinomycete level in the soil. Topdressing with other organic matter such as compost, peat humus and topsoil will do the same. Applications of liquid seaweed have been shown to reduce diseases such as fusarium and dollar spot.

Finally, the secret is to stop treating your lawn as something separate from the rest of your yard. Think of it as a garden of grass. If you have weeds in your lawn, pull or chop them. If disease strikes, find out why and eliminate the cause. If insects move in, don't panic: accept some damage and then use safe biological controls if necessary.

WARREN SCHULTZ *is author of* The Chemical-Free Lawn *(Rodale Press, 1989).*

8 Steps to a Pesticide-Free Lawn

BY WARREN SCHULTZ

||||||||||||||||||||||||||||||||||||||||||||||||||||||||||||||

Going cold turkey is the best way to break your lawn's chemical habit. The sooner you remove harsh chemicals from the diet, the faster the soil will recover. And like any kind of gardening, the key to a trouble-free, sustainable lawn is a healthy soil, thriving with beneficial organisms. You may see some signs of withdrawal at first, but be patient. Here's an eight-step program for easing the transition to a chemical-free lawn.

A lawn aerator rejuvenates the soil so that worms and other soil life can thrive.

WARREN SCHULTZ

Aerate the turf.

Old, well worn lawns often suffer from soil compaction. This is especially the case for chemically maintained turf, because soil life is at a standstill and the soil-aerating activity of earthworms and microorganisms has slowed. Like any plant, grass suffers in compacted soil. Aerating the soil gives it a fresh start. You can buy a hand-and-foot-powered aerator that has four hollow tines that you force into the ground, or rent a power aerator to do the job more quickly.

2

Topdress.

After aerating is an ideal time to topdress the turf. You have all those holes in your lawn; how about filling them with some vital soil or organic matter? Topdressing is a common (and frequent) practice among groundskeepers but one that remains a mystery to homeowners. It simply means covering the turf with a thin (1/8 to 1/4 inch deep) layer of sand, soil or organic matter. For the transitional lawn, it's best to resuscitate the soil with a dose of screened compost. Weed-free topsoil will also do.

Above: An array of lawn weeding tools.
Below: Freshly mowed lawn.

3

Overseed.

If your lawn is more than ten years old then it is handicapped by old-fashioned grass. New varieties are tougher, more vigorous, better looking, drought tolerant, disease and even insect resistant. Find a blend that meets your requirements, then sow it at 1-1/2 times the recommended rate, right over your current turf. If you've just topdressed,

fresh soil will provide an ideal seedbed. If not, scratch the turf roughly with a metal rake before sowing.

4

Fertilize lightly with natural turf food.

Natural fertilizer such as chicken manure or compost-based turf food can add essential disease-fighting microorganisms (such as actinomycetes) as well as all the NPK (nitrogen/phosphorus/potassium, the major components of fertilizer) and micronutrients necessary. Twenty five pounds of chicken manure per 1,000 square feet of lawn, once a year should be all that's necessary.

Above: A weed popper goes to work on a pesky dandelion.

5

Mow high, mow often, leave the clippings.

As they break down on the soil, grass clippings can contribute more than one pound of useable nitrogen per 1,000 square feet. Clippings will begin to break down within one week if the soil is alive with organisms. The breakdown will be slower in a system with a chemical history. In that situation, the smaller the clippings the better. So mow lightly and often or use a mulching mower.

Monitor your lawn.

Take the time to get to know your turf. Look for insects at ground level, or pull back patches of sod to look for grubs underneath. If you find brown or dying patches, before treating for disease, consider environmental causes such as improper drainage, gasoline or pesticide spills, soil compaction or dog damage.

Use biological controls only as necessary.

Your lawn does not need to be a bug-free zone. Take action against pests only if damage is evident and obvious. Then use the most selective, least harmful pesticide available for the job.

Above: Out comes the dandelion, taproot and all.

Consider grass substitutes.

Most disease and weed problems occur where conditions are not conducive to good grass growth. Think about substitutes in those situations, such as ground covers in shady spots or bark or gravel in pathways or heavily trafficked areas.

Turf Tips

RECOMMENDED GRASSES FOR EVERY REGION

ZONE ONE — NORTHEAST AND UPPER MIDWEST

Kentucky Bluegrass	Midnight, Liberty, America, Blacksburg
Perennial Ryegrass	Yorktown II, Palmer, Repell, Pennfine
Tall Fescue	Mustang, Silverado, Rebel II, Olympic
Fine Fescue	Spartan, Reliant, Atlanta
Zoysia	Midwestern

ZONE TWO — SOUTH

Bahiagrass	Paraguay, Pensacola, Argentine
Bermudagrass	Tifgreen, Tifway, Vamont
Zoysia	Meyer, Emerald
Centipedegrass	Oaklawn, Tennessee Hardy
St. Augustinegrass	Roselawn, Better Blue, Floratine
Fine Fescue	Spartan, Reliant, Aurora

ZONE THREE — PLAINS

Buffalograss	Texoka, Prairie, Sharp's Improved
Kentucky Bluegrass	America, Dawn, Harmony
Tall Fescue	Apache, Rebel, Clemfine
Fine Fescue	Reliant, Aurora
Perennial Ryegrass	Blazer, Palmer, Yorktown II
Bermudagrass	Tifway, Tifgreen

GRASS ZONES OF THE UNITED STATES

The United States is divided into five grass zones: the humid Northeast (zone 1), the humid South (zone 2), the Plains (zone 3), the arid Southwest (zone 4) and the humid Northwest (zone 5).

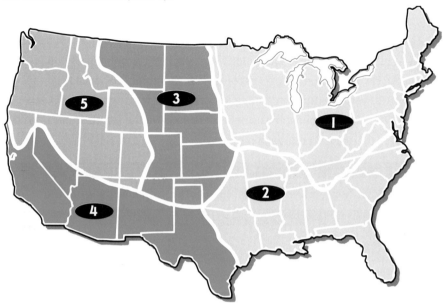

ZONE FOUR	SOUTHWEST
Buffalograss	Texoka, Prairie, Sharp's Improved
Bermudagrass	Tifway II, Tifgreen, Midirion
Tall Fescue	Arid, Apache, Mustang
Perennial Ryegrass	Palmer, Citation II, Tara
Kentucky Bluegrass	Classic, Glade, Trenton
Fine Fescue	Waldina, Scaldis
Zoysia	

ZONE FIVE	NORTHWEST
Kentucky Bluegrass	Blacksburg, Challenger, Midnight
Bentgrass	Exeter, Putter, Prominent
Tall Fescue	Falcon, Houndog, Mustang
Fine Fescue	Reliant, Scaldis, Enjoy
Perennial Ryegrass	Palmer, Manhattan II, Repell

THE LAZY GARDENER'S GUIDE TO
FERTILIZING LAWN

When to fertilize, and how much, depends on where you live and the kind of grass you're growing. Remember, the more you fertilize, the more your grass will grow and the more you'll have to mow. The following is a minimal maintenance schedule for all five grass zones. Recommendations are in actual pounds of nitrogen per 1,000 square feet. To calculate the number of pounds of nitrogen in, say a 40-pound bag of 10-3-4 fertilizer, multiply 40 (what the bag weighs) by 10 percent (the percentage of nitrogen, represented by the first number of the nitrogen-phosphorus-potassium ratio on the fertilizer bag). In other words, there are 4 pounds of nitrogen.

ZONE 1	THE HUMID NORTHEAST

Two pounds in September or October or after grass stops growing

ZONE 2	THE HUMID SOUTH

For Summer Grasses*
> One pound in June, one pound in August

For Winter Grasses*
> Two pounds in September or October

ZONE 3	THE PLAINS

Two pounds in September

ZONE 4	THE ARID SOUTHWEST

For Summer Grasses, Cool-Season Species*, Irrigated
> 1-1/2 pounds in October or November, 1-1/2 in May or June

For Summer Grasses, Warm-Season Species*, Irrigated
> 1/2 pound every month, May to August

For Summer Grasses, Warm-Season Species, Non-Irrigated
> One pound in April or May, one pound August

For Winter Grasses, Cool-Season Species
> Two pounds in October or November

ZONE 5	THE HUMID NORTHWEST

Two pounds in October or November or after the grass stops growing

* In southern regions, warm-season species such as Bermudagrass or Bahiagrass are the summer grasses of choice. They are sometimes overseeded in fall with a cool season species such as Kentucky bluegrass or ryegrass that provides winter green after the summer grass has gone dormant.

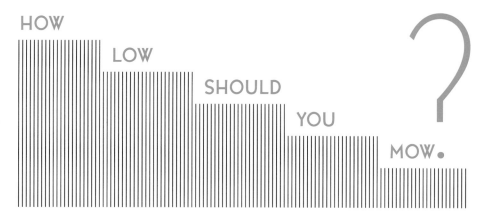

HOW LOW SHOULD YOU MOW.?

Mowing is probably the most important thing you do to your lawn. Most people mow much too low. Mowing high is the key to a healthy lawn. Here are the best mowing heights in inches, by species. As indicated, the mower deck should be raised in hot weather or shade, and lowered somewhat for the last mow before winter.

COOL-SEASON GRASSES	COOL WEATHER AND/OR SHADE	HOT WEATHER	LAST MOW
Bentgrass	1/3	2/3	1/3
Kentucky bluegrass	2-1/2	3	2
Fine fescue	1-1/2	2-1/2	1
Tall fescue	2-1/2	4	2
Perennial ryegrass	1-1/2	2-1/2	1

WARM-SEASON GRASSES	COOL WEATHER AND/OR SHADE	HOT WEATHER	LAST MOW
Bahiagrass	2	3	1-1/2
Bermudagrass	1/2	1	1/2
Buffalograss	1-1/2	2-1/2	1
Centipedegrass	1	2	1
St. Augustinegrass	2	3	1-1/2
Zoysia	1/2	1	1/2

Adapted from The Chemical Free Lawn *by Warren Schultz (Rodale Press, 1989)*

Building Better Grass Seeds

Growing a lawn from the new breeds of seed makes being an organic gardener a whole lot easier

BY MARIE POMPEI

The turfgrass industry has come a long way. Just a few decades ago, grass selection for a handsome lawn pretty much began and ended with Kentucky bluegrass in the North and Bermudagrass in the South. These lawns would do well only if they were lavished with fertilizer, water and pesticides.

The alternatives also left a lot to be desired. Perennial ryegrasses were coarse and unattractive, difficult to mow and short lived. Tall fescues were so coarse-looking that they were used strictly for forage or on steep banks where their strong, deep roots helped control erosion. The bristle-like fine fescues were considered to be "the shade grass" and used only as a component of shade mixtures.

But today, when you look for grass seed you can choose from scores of improved varieties that have a pleasing dark green color, finer texture and disease and insect resistance without so much chemical help. They also have better mowability, meaning that you get a cleaner cut, without shredding the leaf.

Grass Bugs Refuse to Eat

One of the most dramatic developments has been the introduction of new, insect-resistant lawngrasses. For example, perennial ryegrass varieties such as Palmer II, Repell II and Citation II have improved insect resistance thanks to a naturally occurring fungus found in the plant called an endophyte. The plant is inoculated with endophyte, which becomes concentrated in the stem and crown portion. The fungus is most effective in repelling insects that feed on these areas of the plant, including aphids, armyworms, billbugs, chinch bugs and sod webworms. Endophytes are transmitted by seed only; they don't spread from plant to plant in the field. And because endophytes are a living fungus, they will die after one year if the seed is not stored properly. When purchasing endophyte-enhanced seed, look for seed labeled for that year and store unused portions in a cool (40 degrees F is ideal), dry spot out of direct sunlight.

Species other than perennial ryegrass also have endophyte-enhanced varieties. Turf-type tall fescues such as Titan, Shenandoah, Tribute and Mesa contain the fungus, as do the fine fescue varieties Jamestown II Chewings fescue, Reliant hard fescue and Warwick. There are no known varieties of Kentucky bluegrass or creeping bentgrass that are endophyte enhanced; however, research is ongoing in this area.

Studies have also shown that endophyte-enhanced varieties are more tolerant of heat and drought. Researchers are currently looking at a link between endophytes and disease incidence as well.

Weed Alert

Some of the grasses mentioned in this article grow so readily that they have become pernicious pests in natural areas, crowding out native species. John Randall, "weed czar" of the Nature Conservancy, which operates scores of nature preserves across the country, reports that tall fescue is extremely invasive in moist areas of the West, particularly east Texas and Oklahoma, Arkansas, Idaho, Oregon and Ohio. Kentucky bluegrass (native to North Africa and Eurasia, not the Bluegrass State) is a problem in the Midwest; perennial ryes in California. If you live near a natural area, be sure to consult the park or preserve manager about invasive grasses and other plants you should avoid growing in your garden.

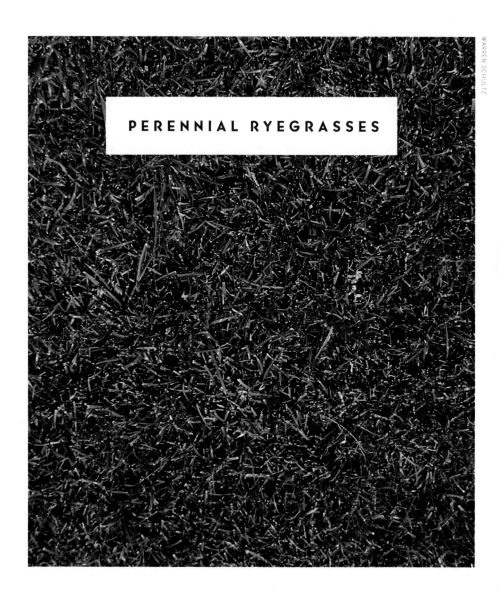

PERENNIAL RYEGRASSES

Breeders have not only made the perennial ryegrasses unpalatable to insects, but they've also greatly improved their color and general appearance. The color of newly released Palmer II, Prelude II, Yorktown III and Repell II is dark and very attractive. That means less fertilizer will have to be applied to these varieties during the year to maintain a pleasing color.

Finer texture and improved mowability are other pluses of these varieties, and they're much quicker to become established. Their slower and lower growth means you spend less time behind the mower and generate fewer clippings that need to be disposed of.

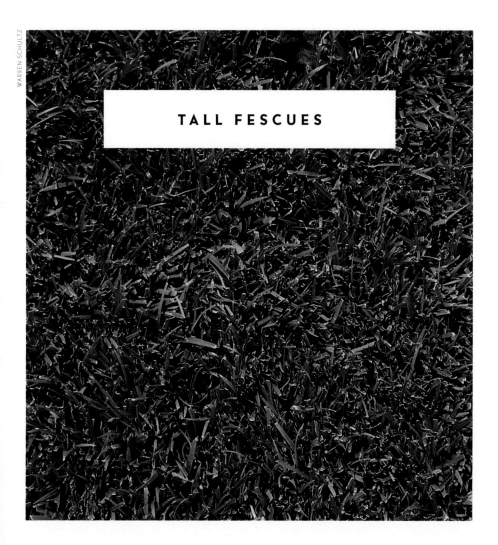

TALL FESCUES

Kentucky 31-type tall fescues were the only game in town until 1980 when Rebel hit the market. Since then there has been an explosion of new turf-type tall fescue varieties — over 60 in all. These new improved cultivars not only are heat and drought tolerant but they also have a finer texture and darker green color than Kentucky 31.

Tall fescues are supremely useful in the landscape as they are adapted to both shady and sunny locations and tolerate a wide range of soil conditions. They're generally tough grasses and extremely wear tolerant once established. Furthermore, they need less nitrogen than Kentucky bluegrass or perennial ryegrass. And, as already mentioned, some varieties are endophyte enhanced for improved insect resistance.

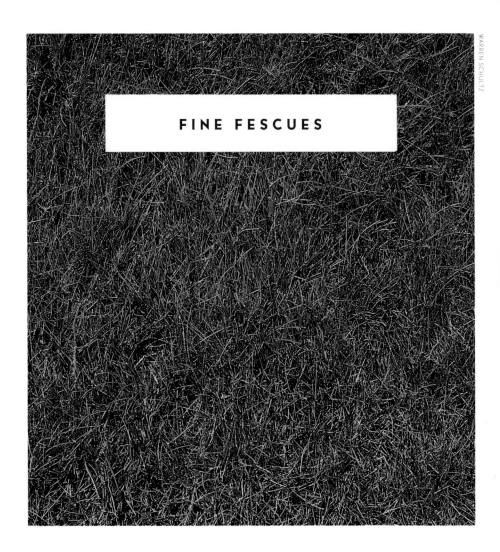

FINE FESCUES

The fine fescues, including Chewings fescue, hard fescue, creeping red fescue and sheep fescue, are finally receiving their due. Known for years for their shade tolerance, these attractive, fine-textured grasses are also increasingly being hailed for their low-maintenance requirements. They reach a mature height of only 12 to 18 inches, don't like a lot of fertilizer and tolerate droughty soil. They work well on slopes or any area that is difficult to mow and maintain. When left unmown, fine fescues do well in sun or shade. If you prefer a more controlled look, only two mowings are needed per year: one in mid to late June and again in late September, both to a height of 4 inches. Varieties to look for include Jamestown II Chewings fescue, Reliant hard fescue, Warwick and SR5000 Chewings fescue. Many of these varieties are enhanced with endophytes for insect resistance.

KENTUCKY BLUEGRASS

Kentucky bluegrass is still the king of turfgrasses for many homeowners and landscapers, thanks to its fine-textured, deep green blades and its ability to spread quickly to form a dense sod. Yet not all varieties of Kentucky bluegrass are easy to maintain. Fortunately, many new lower-maintenance varieties that require less moisture and fertilizer are now available, including Midnight, Ram I, Merit and Baron.

When it's time to reseed or renovate your lawn, be sure to look for a mix that includes these new, improved varieties — or mix your own, using the grasses best suited to the conditions in your yard.

MARIE POMPEI, *a research agronomist with Lofts Seed, Inc., is involved in all phases of turfgrass research, including the coordination of university testing of new varieties introduced by the company.*

37

How to Renovate Your Lawn

What to do when it's time to start over

BY MARIA T. CINQUE

The best time to completely renovate a lawn is when temperatures are cool and rain is plentiful. In the Northeast, this is between mid-August and the end of September; in this part of the country, late-summer seeding is preferable to springtime seeding because it is generally warmer and the new grass has almost a whole year to grow before it is subject to summer heat and drought. What's more, there's far less competition from weeds.

Get Rid of the Existing Grass

The first order of business is to remove all the existing turf. Dig up the grass or till it under. Rake up and remove the clumps. Be sure to dig deeply enough to remove the entire root of persistent, deep-rooted weeds like dandelions. If the existing lawn is full of hard-to-kill perennial weeds like quack grass you can spray a non-selective herbicide on the old lawn. This will eliminate not only the weeds but any existing grass. Consult your local Cooperative Extension office for the name of the safest one to use. Keep in mind that a non-selective herbicide by definition will kill most plants it comes in contact with, so if there is anything you don't want to eliminate, don't allow the spray to get on it. Don't spray in the wind or rain and read and follow the instructions and precautions on the label. After the grass is dead rake it up.

The best time to renovate your lawn is when temperatures are cool and rain is plentiful. In this case, simple spot seeding should do the trick. Use a heavy metal rake to remove the thatch and clippings and expose the soil.

Add Organic Matter, Lime and Fertilizer

Adequate soil drainage is a prerequisite to having a healthy lawn. Water shouldn't puddle up after a rainfall. Conversely, very sandy soils often drain too fast and your grass will easily become stressed from lack of moisture. You can remedy both kinds of drainage problems by adding organic matter to your existing soil. Unless the problem is severe, a 4- to 6-inch layer of compost or peat moss mixed into the top 8 to 10 inches of soil should help to alleviate most drainage difficulties. Compost has advantages over peat moss: it is usually readily available at little or no cost from recycling centers, or you can buy it at the local garden center. Many people have their own composting bins which serve not only as a source of organic matter but also as a way to recycle garden trimmings.

Even if you don't have severe drainage problems, your soil may need some organic matter. You can tell by its appearance. If it is very sandy or very clayey,

 *(JUDY WHITE)*

One way to get rid of your old lawn is to cover it with plastic until all of the grass is dead.

chances are the organic content is not good enough. If there's time, have your soil tested to determine the level of organic matter.

If possible, establish a soil grade that slopes slightly away from the house or other buildings. Avoid steep slopes because they are difficult to establish and mow. When regrading, keep in mind that soil added on top of tree or shrub roots can cause injury to the plants.

Lawn grasses prefer the soil pH in the 6.5 to 7.0 range. This is very important because essential turfgrass nutrients are most available to the grass at this pH. Inexpensive soil pH test kits are available at most nurseries. If the soil pH is below 6.5, add lime to bring it up to the proper level.

Seed sown on unfertilized soils usually produces a thin and unhealthy turf. While you're adding lime and organic matter, incorporate the proper amount of a complete fertilizer into the top 6 to 8 inches of your soil. Use a fertilizer with plenty of phosphorus. (Phosphorus is the middle number on the fertilizer bag.)

The same lawn after renovation. A stone wall and shrubs have eliminated a hard-to-mow slope.

Because phosphorus moves very slowly in the soil, it must be mixed into the soil to be effective, not just sprinkled on top.

Mix the organic matter, lime and fertilizer into the soil by rototilling or spading. You can rent a rototiller or hire a landscape gardener to do this.

A level seedbed is an absolute must. Rake the entire area with a wide wooden or aluminum rake. It's a good idea to allow a few days for the ground to settle before the final raking so that high and low spots can be eliminated.

Before you seed, add another light application of fertilizer to make sure there is adequate fertilizer near the germinating seed.

Sow the Seed

If you're preparing your own seed mix, make sure that all the varieties of grasses are evenly distributed throughout the mixture. For this reason, it's usually best to buy a commercial seed blend that has been mixed by the manufacturer.

A level seedbed is an absolute must. Rake the entire area with a wide wooden or aluminum rake. Seed, then rake again lightly — just enough to cover the seed with 1/8 inch of soil.

Divide the grass seed in half and sow half the mixture in one direction and the other half at right angles to it.

Lightly rake the seedbed just enough to cover the seeds with about 1/8 inch of soil. Don't rake too deeply — if the seeds are covered with too much soil, they may not germinate.

You may want to consider rolling the seedbed with a light roller to firm the soil and promote better seed-soil contact, which in turn will promote better seed germination. Deleting this step will not harm the seed, but it may germinate a little more slowly.

Water is critical when you're getting your new stand of grass established, even if the grass is a drought-tolerant type. Don't overwater or the seeds may wash away. Water lightly but enough so that the top few inches of soil are moist. After this initial watering, water lightly several times a day, especially on hot, windy days. Try not to walk over the newly seeded area. As soon as the grass is three inches high, mow it. Your new lawn should be mowed regularly from then on. ▥

MARIA T. CINQUE *is a turfgrass specialist and coordinator of turfgrass research for Cornell Cooperative Extension on Long Island, New York.*

SPOT SEEDING

If your lawn has a few bare spots, your task is a lot easier. Mow the lawn very closely, then use a heavy metal rake to remove thatch and clippings and expose the soil. With a hoe or spade, remove major weeds. Selective herbicides (herbicides that kill only specific types of weeds) can be used for weed control, but you'll have to wait at least a month to seed the bare spots after making the application; consult your local Cooperative Extension office about which herbicide to use.

Seed, rake lightly, topdress with a thin layer of compost or soil and water well.

JUDY WHITE

Buffalograss

The greatest contribution to weekend leisure time since the invention of remote-control TV

BY SALLY WASOWSKI

WITH ANDY WASOWSKI

*J*ust when I thought I was inured to reading shocking revelations about celebrities, I came upon this tidbit in my local paper. It seems that actor Richard Widmark was quoted in *Architectural Digest* as admitting to "a passion for cutting grass." He not only mows his own 40-acre Connecticut estate, he then tackles the lawns of his neighbors. He claims to find this ... "very satisfying."

No wonder this made the papers. All the people I know who enjoy mowing their lawns could fit into my car, and

Left: Female buffalograss showing non-pollen producing flower. Right: Male buffalograss showing prominent pollen-producing flower. Female is best for a consistent green lawn.

DR M C ENGELKE

Prairie buffalograss lawn on right; Bermuda on left. The Bermudagrass received over 30 waterings that year; the buffalograss only two.

still leave room for three suitcases, two stereo speakers and an 8-gallon ice-chest.

Which is why, someday, there may well be a movement to canonize Drs. M. C. Engelke and Terry Riordan, and Virginia Lehman.

These three people are responsible for perhaps the greatest contribution to weekend leisure time since the invention of remote control TV. They have been pioneers in the development of a lawn that can be mowed as few as one to four times a year and still look impeccable. This miracle lawn is composed of new varieties of a native American plant called buffalograss *(Buchloe dactyloides)* that grow to a maximum of only 4 to 6 inches — and then stop!

The new buffalograsses are fine-textured, extremely heat- and cold-resistant and drought-tolerant, and require minimal fertilization and pesticide control. They spread quickly and green up earlier in the spring than St. Augustine or Bermuda. Female varieties offer an additional bonus for hayfever sufferers; because they lack the distinctive male flowers found on other strains of buffalo-grass, there is no pollen. To keep them all-female, best for a consistent green lawn, the grasses must be planted by sprigs, plugs or sod, instead of seed.

Dr. Engelke, at the Texas A&M Experiment Station in Dallas, and his student, Virginia Lehman, were responsible for one of the earliest buffalograsses, 'Prairie', which posseses a soft "apple green" color. Dr. Riordan, working at the

The same lawns, showing winter colors — the buffalograss has a softer, more golden hue.

University of Nebraska, developed '609', which hit the market a few months after 'Prairie', and is touted as having a somewhat darker, blue-green color and a denser mat. Both turf grasses instantly found an enthusiastic market.

Interest in buffalograss for lawns developed among water-conscious homeowners in the Southwest at least ten years ago. Aside from its drought tolerance, wild buffalograss is as close to a natural lawn as anything I have ever seen; it is genetically low-growing.

But back then, the only kinds available to buy were tall and had to be planted from seed. The most commonly used varieties were 'Texoca' and 'Sharp's Improved'; both were bred for use in pastures and grow to about a foot high.

Buffalograss is native throughout the Great Plains, from Minnesota to Montana and south into Mexico — growing wherever conditions aren't too moist, too dry (deep sand) or too shady. It takes extreme cold (minus 30 degrees F) and lots of heat (plus 120 degrees F). It is a warm-season grass that tends to be green from early spring to late fall. But it can turn golden brown, that is, go dormant and send all its juices down to its roots for safekeeping, whenever it needs to protect itself from either extreme drought or extreme cold.

Buffalograss has a fine, soft, even texture that invites bare feet. At the same time, it takes a lot of foot traffic without complaining. It covers quickly, outlives

standard turf grasses, needs less fertilizer to remain dense and forms such a tight sod that weeds can't get a root in edgewise. Another nice thing — it is not at all attracted to the rich, moist environment of your flowerbed, where it is not wanted.

In fact, there is only one thing that can make a buffalograss lawn look bad, and that is *too much water*. Buffalograss's worst enemy is the well-meaning homeowner or groundskeeper who insists on treating it like conventional grass — by drowning it.

This buffalograss lawn, sown by broadcasting the seed, is barely a year old. The bed of native wildflowers includes winecups and red yucca.

No wonder water departments all over the country are enthusiastic fans of buffalograss; it fits in perfectly with the new xeriscape (low water-use) concept of landscaping that many of them are promoting.

Buffalograss needs 25 to 30 percent less water than common Bermuda, approximately 80 percent less than hybrid Bermuda, 75 percent less than Kentucky bluegrass and 50 to 80 percent less than St. Augustine. Dr. David Northington, Director of the National Wildflower Research Center in Austin, Texas, tells the story of when he went off on vacation one year and didn't water his buffalograss lawn at all during July and August. When he returned home, his lawn was greener than his neighbor's Bermuda lawn, which had been watered twice a week.

Because it needs little or no water, little or no fertilizer and little mowing, a buffalograss lawn is a cinch to maintain. Its primary requirement is lots of sunlight, making it ideal for golf courses, schools, parks, dams, roadsides, public buildings and suburban corporate headquarters — and, of course, residences that aren't covered up by shade trees.

Buffalograss support, not surprisingly, comes mostly from its own native territory — the West and Midwest — where it provides folks with the low-maintenance lawn they've always wanted but until now didn't believe was possible. But interest in buffalograss is spreading beyond its native range, with some of the newer varieties being tested and used throughout much of the United States.

In Los Alamitos, California, 'Prairie' buffalograss is credited with making the Cypress Golf Course possible. Tom Buzbee, with Kajima Engineering and Construction, Inc., says that the course had only 100 acres available to work with — much less than on the average golf course. Fitting in all eighteen holes while keeping golfers from killing each other with misdirected slices and hooks called for a creative display of earth-moving and mound-building, effectively protecting one fairway from the others without resorting to unsightly, artificial fences and screens.

The result was a series of precipitous slopes that were a maintenance crew's nightmare. The buffalograss was installed and mowing was reduced to just once every five to six weeks. Common Bermuda must be mowed once every five days! And don't forget the umpteen million gallons of water that will be saved over the lifetime of the course.

Dr. David Huff, assistant professor of plant genetics at Rutgers University in New Jersey, gives buffalograss a qualified thumbs up for the Northeast, and says it does well in dry, compacted, heavy soils. According to Huff, there is great interest in using buffalograss along both the New Jersey Turnpike and the Garden State Parkway, on steep, unmowable slopes.

Dr. Huff is also working on a short-leaved buffalograss from Mexico, a diploid that should deliver still greater density — and an all-male short turf variety that comes with different colored anthers (the parts of the flower in which pollen is produced); he already has red, white and blue separated. Imagine that growing in the front lawn of the White House!

As for Mr. Widmark ... well, I don't think he'll be ordering any for his home in the near future.

SALLY WASOWSKI *is a Dallas-based landscape designer and author. Her latest book, coauthored with her husband,* ANDY WASOWSKI, *a free-lance writer and photographer, is* Requiem for a Lawnmower *(Taylor Publishing).*

The Lawnless Landscape

How to stand tall and throw off the yoke of turfgrass tyranny — and remain friends with your neighbors

BY SALLY WASOWSKI

WITH ANDY WASOWSKI

A few years back, Sara Lowen wrote a wonderful article for *American Heritage* magazine which addressed our seemingly slavish devotion to surrounding our homes with carpets of turf grass. She called her piece, "The Tyranny of the Lawn." In fact, the title could just as easily have been, "The Tyranny of the Neighbors."

Worrying about what the neighbors will think is basic to being *homo sapiens*, like walking erect and paying taxes. Remember back in high school? Getting the approval of our peers was more important than food.

Today, we're sophisticated, logical adults, but we still insist on spending an inordinate amount of time pushing a lawnmower around our property (or paying out good money to have some kid do it). Worse, we coddle our grass — annointing it with oceans of water and toxic chemicals. If the grass is always greener in the other guy's yard ... it drives us absolutely nuts!

If we happen to live in a part of the country that has periodic, even chronic, water shortages (and that means most of us), we see nothing wrong with running our sprinkler systems full blast, even at high noon during the summer's worst heat. Andy and I have driven through neighborhoods in the southwestern deserts, where rainfall is measured in fractions of an inch, and seen the kind of lush lawns one expects to find in, say, Virginia or New England.

Left: The authors' home, the August after they got rid of the last of their lawn. This environmentally friendly landscape uses little water, no chemicals and requires only a few days per year of maintenance. Wildflowers spill onto a limestone path.

Aside from the unconscionable waste of precious water, these landscapes have no "sense of place." They contribute to the homogenizing of America, where a neighborhood in Ohio looks pretty much like a neighborhood in Georgia or California. We seem, also, to be losing a sense of time; our dependence on evergreenery, including turf grasses, such as winter rye, gives many of our landscapes a mind-numbing, uni-seasonal appearance.

VIOLA MISSOURIENSIS, Missouri violet

And why? Because we don't want our neighbors to think ill of us. As humorist Dave Berry so pointedly put it, "In America, having a nice lawn is considered a major cultural achievement, like owning a hardcover book or watching 'Meet the Press.' The average American would rather live next door to a pervert-heroin addict-Communist-pornographer than someone with an unkempt lawn."

But while this typical landscape of lawn, evergreen boxhedge and some trash trees may be neat, it's also boring. Worse, it's a lot of work! In fact, I've formulated an axiom, based on years of personal observation: "The more boring the landscape, the greater the need for upkeep and maintenance." Check me out on that.

If you are nodding agreement as you read this, yet you are still maintaining such a landscape, then it's time for you to stand tall and throw off the yoke of turfgrass tyranny. It's time for you to convert your landscape to a more natural-looking, low-maintenance, environmentally friendly scene.

Does this mean you should totally disregard your neighbors' feelings? Not at all. It's important to maintain good relations; you never know when you'll need to drop over and borrow a cup of sugar or an extension cord or something. Therefore, unless you are unusually courageous, start off subtly. We did, and most of our neighbors are not only still talking to us, but a few have actually started imitating us.

PHLOX PILOSA, fragrant phlox

When we first moved into our present home fifteen years ago, the front yard was just another conventional landscape. But that was okay — we were still fairly conventional in those days, too. The lawn was St. Augustine, an especially bad choice for most of the Southwest because it doesn't just drink water; it guzzles it. So, naturally, we did what the neighbors had done — we put in a sprinkler system.

In those days, I was still a lay gardener — and a blackthumb one at that. The reason I'd loved wildflowers all my life was because they survived my care better than anything else.

Soon after moving in, I began hearing how some people were using native ornamental trees and shrubs in the landscape instead of the same old standard nursery stock. These natives, it was rumored, required far less coddling; after all, they had survived in these parts for millenia with no help from anyone. These sounded like my kind of plants.

About this time, too, I was beginning to play around with landscape designs — for myself at first, then for a few family members and friends. Incredibly, one day my cousin Jenny offered to pay me for a plan. I was off and running in a new career.

And because I had decided to specialize in natives, I needed an experimental garden where I could try out plants before recommending them to my trusting clients. The front of our property, along the street, was so designated.

Back then, just finding native plants was a chore! Your average nursery was as ignorant of native plants as were their customers. I did a lot of seed collecting in vacant lots, and saved a few plants that would otherwise have been bulldozed under. And, in some instances, I drove down to Austin, home of one of the very few nurseries that actually specialized in natives at that time.

TRADESCANTIA SP., spiderwort

Each new addition to my garden was carefully hand-watered, giving it just enough the first year to get it established. After that, watering was minimal, and then only to bring out the best the plants had to offer. I not only wanted them to look better than they do in the wild; I wanted them to look gorgeous; I wanted them to wow my neighbors.

The St. Augustine lawn, by the way, got just as little water as the native garden, and we expected to see it dry up and die. It didn't. Partly because it was in a semi-shady area, partly because it had been so well established and partly, I think, just to spite me and my new gardening ideas, it hung in there year after year.

But it was the native garden that was the focus of my landscape; and I was delighted when passing joggers would pant a compliment about the colorful seasonal displays. Of course, in the back of my mind, one nagging question still lurked — was my experimental garden acceptable to the neighbors only because I still maintained a lawn — albeit a small one? Was it possible that this grassy patch made all my native planting "tolerable?"

If so, I would soon put them to a real test.

In my design business, many of my customers were people who had purchased undeveloped land out beyond the suburbs — land that had not yet been scraped clean by a bulldozer. Here, I was able to design truly natural landscapes, building on the wonderful raw materials Mother Nature had placed there. The

RUELLIA SP., ruellia

concept was simple: the house should look like it had been gently set down into the landscape. The hand of the designer should be seen only in a subtle way.

I loved this natural look, and began to wonder why it couldn't be re-created on established landscapes, such as my own. Would it be possible to undo that "civilized," over-controlled look that so many of us were living with? My husband and I decided to find out. We would eliminate that lawn altogether. Our front yard would display not one blade of conventional turfgrass. Instead, it would be designed with a palette of plants that would make it look like a natural woodland.

Now, the purist in me wanted to rip out everything that was not indigenous to Dallas. I would have loved the challenge of re-creating an authentic Dallas woods, such as might have originally been on the creek bank that our lot once was.

What seemed more sensible for my garden was to build on what I already had — and that included many non-native plants that I had inherited along with the deed. Whatever could survive my watering regimen and lack of pampering, I figured, had earned the right to stay. All except the lawn, that is! That got plowed under. Then I added three native flowering understory trees — an Eve's necklace *(Sophora affinis)*, a rusty blackhaw viburnum *(Viburnum rufidulum)* and a Mexican buckeye *(Ungnadia speciosa)* — and created a knee-high groundcover of native and near-native plants — horseherb *(Calyptocarpus vialis)*, avens *(Geum* canadense), Turk's cap (*Malvaviscus arboreus* var. *drummondii)* and a polite but unidentified sedge - most of which were already here in abundance and only needed to be divided and transplanted.

Winding up from the street to the front gate is a walkway of limestone slabs. A second limestone path crosses at the top, coming from the neighbor's yard, and meets the first path. This second path is more pragmatic than aesthetic; that's the route the mailman takes.

LONICERA SEMPERVIRENS, **coral honeysuckle**

As I write this, in early January, the yard looks its worst. It is brown and dormant. Fallen leaves are beginning to decompose, bringing natural nourishment to the soil. But notice, I said it looks its worst — I did *not* say it looks ugly. There is real beauty here. The low morning sun hits the inland seaoats (*Chasmanthium latifolium*), making the seedheads glow golden and bringing out hints of purple in the dark yellow stalks. Patches of green showing along the path and amidst the fallen leaves are tufts of native sedge and the leafy rosettes of various herbs and wildflowers, such as avens, greeneyes *(Berlandiera texana)* and obedient plant *(Physostegia virginiana)*.

In February, my natural garden starts off with a sprinkling of Missouri violets *(Viola missouriensis* — ours are palest lavender with purple markings) and crow poison *(Nothoscordum bivalve)*, both of which are in abundance in the older woodland on the other side of my driveway. In April, things really get exciting. On the back wall are two vines. First to bloom is sweet-smelling Carolina jessamine *(Gelsemium sempervirens)* and then the hummingbird-tempting coral honeysuckle *(Lonicera sempervirens)*. In wet years, these are accompanied by wild red columbines *(Aguilegia canadensis)* and the dainty white fringe of meadow rue *(Thalictrum dasycarpum)*. Always, there are two kinds of ruellia *(Ruellia* spp.), one lavender and one purple, two kinds of spiderwort (*Tradescantia* spp.), one grasslike and blue and the other more upright and purple, and my beloved *Phlox pilosa* that perfumes the air. By mid-spring, there are Louisiana irises, also in shades of blue, lavender, purple and cerise.

I usually weed twice during this period. The first time, I pull out all the pecan trees that the squirrels planted the previous fall. The second time, I laboriously dig out all the pecan trees I missed the first time.

As the weather gets hotter, the garden moves into its summer mode. The grassy spiderwort continues to bloom. A cultivar of wild hydrangea *(Hydrangea arborescens)* raises its white heads, and the tiny white strawberrylike blooms of avens float through the garden. Then, the yellow daisies come into dominance. Greeneyes *(Berlandiera texana)* with its soft, fuzzy leaves and green centers is my favorite, but I am also exceedingly fond of zexmenia *(Wedelia hispida)*. It forms a

SALVIA ROEMERIANA, **cedar sage**

MALVAVISCUS ARBOREUS var. DRUMMONDII, **turk's cap**

ground cover of scattered gold. Lanceleaf coreopsis *(Coreopsis lanceolata)* is followed by black-eyed Susans *(Rudbeckia hirta)*.

Mid-summer is when the hummingbirds come to my garden and stay until fall. To greet them are Turk's cap *(Malvaviscus arboreus* var. *drummondii)* with their red hibiscuslike flowers that never quite open, and trumpet vine *(Campsis radicans)* with its big, orange, bell-shaped blooms. Also, there are four kinds of native sages *(Salvia engelmannia, S. roemeriana, S. coccinea* and *S. greggii)* — one blue and three red. These bloomed in the spring also, but their flowers always seem more significant this time of year. Cool white summer phlox (*Phlox paniculata*) gets an occasional visit, but seems more popular with the butterflies.

Maintenance at this time of year amounts to picking up a beer can discarded by some passing yahoo. It's too hot to do anything more, and the flowers are so thick, no weed has a

WEDELIA HISPIDA, **zexmenia**

BERLANDIERA TEXANA, **greeneyes**

chance anyway.

As the weather begins to cool down into the 80s, at least at night, the fall flowers add lavender tones to the reds of summer. Wild ageratum (*Eupatorium coelestinum*) and fall obedient plant (*Physostegia virginiana*) are the strongest, but the ruellias and spiderworts usually make a comeback. Yellows are provided by the small daisies of zexmenia (which never stopped blooming) and a return of greeneyes.

ANDY &SALLY WASOWSKI

EUPATORIUM COELESTINUM, wild ageratum, mist flower

After a hard freeze, I do the third day of maintenance in my garden. I cut back all the brown, ragged stalks. I weed out all the unwanted plants that arrived during the summer. I transplant and rearrange new seedlings of the flowers that did not place themselves to my aesthetic satisfaction.

The leaves from my trees — bur oak (*Quercus macrocarpa*), chinquapin oak (*Quercus muehlenbergia*), bois d'arc (*Maclura pomifera*), Shumard red oak (*Quercus shumardii*) and American elm (*Ulmus americanus)* — are allowed to stay where they fall, as are the leaves from my neighbor's too-fecund pecan (*Carya illinoinensis*). Occasionally I will uncover a flower rosette buried too far below the mulch. But mostly I just make sure the garden is bedded down under its comforter of leaves for the winter, so it will be healthy and happy and ready to go next spring.

Season after season, year after year, my natural native garden evolves and matures, offering never-ending surprises and visual treats.

I have a recurring nightmare. In it, we sell our house and move away. A year later, we drive through the old neighborhood and pass the house. My natural landscape is no more. A manicured lawn has taken its place. And the new owners are out in their yard mowing and spraying and edging and weeding. And looking very self-righteous.

Made for the Shade

Want a velvety green carpet that you won't have to mow, water, fertilize or spray? Forget about grass. Grow moss

BY DAVID E. BENNER

*T*hirty years ago, my wife and I purchased a shady, two-acre property in southeastern Pennsylvania. The existing grass areas were pathetic and full of weeds. It would be a constant struggle just to a have a decent grass lawn on this sloping wooded terrain, I realized, and mowing would have to be done with a hand mower. Noticing small patches of mosses here and there, I envisioned entire carpets of these velvet-green plants as an alternative.

The author's garden, left and above, features wildflowers, trees, shrubs and entire carpets of velvet-green moss.

Unable to find any book on how to develop a moss lawn, I tried a simple experiment. It worked perfectly. In May 1962, I sprinkled sulfur dust on all grass areas. Six weeks later, most of the grass was dead or dying. Since the soil was already acidic, further acidification with sulfur caused the grass to simply die, along with most of the weeds. Some aluminum sulfate was also added. (A soil pH of 5.0 to 5.5 is ideal for most mosses). By fall of that year, existing moss patches had begun to spread, and new sections were growing where there was once only grass. In less than two years, moss lawns blanketed the property. There are now over twenty-five species growing here; none were planted. For twenty-eight years, there has been no grass!

Mosses are fascinating primitive plants that reproduce by spores (not seeds) that are as fine as dust. These spores can be borne on the wind for hundreds, and probably thousands, of miles. They can land anywhere and

Top left: Moss pathways crisscross the garden. Contrary to popular belief, moss is a tough plant — tougher than grass.

Left: Haircap moss, *Polytrichum commune.*

begin to germinate when subjected to the proper growing conditions. Mosses have no true roots, but rather special structures called rhizoids that help anchor the plants wherever they happen to grow. There are over twenty thousand species of mosses worldwide that can be found from sea level to the highest mountaintops. Mosses obtain water and nutrients through their tiny leaves and stems. Because there is no protective coating on the foliage, the moisture and nutrients are absorbed very quickly. This can be seen after a severe drought, when moss plants appear brown and curled up as if dead. One brief shower, and in less than an hour these same plants are lush and green, like a miracle. Moss is a tough plant — tougher than grass. I give guided tours every spring and people ask me if you can walk on moss. I explain to them that over two-hundred visitors travel on the same moss paths (with flat heels) every year.

Top right: Another moss path ascends to the house. More than 25 species of moss grow in the garden, and nary a blade of grass.

Right: *Thuidium*, top, and *Dicranum*, bottom.

The average moss plant grows from one-half to one and one-half inches in height. The one exception is haircap moss *(Polytrichum commune)*. This is the largest of all mosses, often growing about ten inches tall. It is also one of the most common, with worldwide distribution. Easy to transplant, it will take sun or shade. This is one of the two most abundant on my grounds, creating miniature landscapes with its height and dark green color. The other is fern moss *(Thuidium delicatulum)*, which spreads quickly into large flat mats about one inch high. It has a lovely emerald-green hue and is also easy to transplant.

When thousands of moss spores alight on a soil surface, they look like a thin green film as they germinate and begin to grow. In about a year, you'll have a velvet-green carpet. Weedy plants do not fare well in shady, acid soils, and are crowded out by dense beds of moss. You not only won't have to weed your moss lawn — you won't have to mow, water or fertilize, either.

DAVID E. BENNER *is a landscape designer specializing in naturalistic gardens. He is a former assistant professor of horticulture at Delaware Valley College in Doylestown, Pennsylvania. His property and gardening techniques are featured on a new forty-five minute instructional video entitled Made In The Shade. For more information call 1-800-753-4660.*

Among the masses of wildflowers that accent the carpets of moss are spiky white foamflower and purple creeping phlox.

Evergreen ground covers are great accents with carpets of moss. I now have over forty species and varieties of evergreen ground covers in my garden, planted densely to prevent the growth of weeds. Remember, eliminating bare soil on your property will solve your weed and erosion problems — at least most of them. By featuring wildflowers, native shrubs and trees, as well as moss, you'll have a natural landscape that is attractive year-round. You'll be able to relax and enjoy this woodland setting, because it's practically maintenance free.

My favorite evergreen ground covers are:

NAME	HEIGHT	OUTSTANDING FEATURES
Pachysandra (*Pachysandra terminalis*)	6-12"	foliage
Vinca (*Vinca minor*)	6-8"	foliage, flowers
Foamflower (*Tiarella cordifolia*)	3-6"	flowers
Partridgeberry (*Mitchella repens*)	1"	foliage, flower, fruit
Creeping Phlox (*Phlox stolonifera*)	1"	flowers
Shortia (*Shortia galacifolia*)	2-4"	foliage, flowers
Bluets (*Hedyotis caerulea*)	1/2"	flowers
Christmas Fern (*Polystichum acrostichoides*)	12-18"	foliage

TIPS ON
GROWING MOSS

● Make sure the soil is acid. You can test with a simple pH soil-test kit, available at most garden centers. The soil should be around 5.0 to 5.5. If necessary, add sulfur, ferrous sulfate or aluminum sulfate as follows:

PH TO START	PH DESIRED	POUNDS OF MATERIAL PER 100 SQUARE FEET		
		ALUMINUM SULFATE	FERROUS SULFATE	SULFUR
8.0	5.5	13.5	25.9	5.5
7.5	5.5	11.5	23.5	5.0
7.0	5.5	9.0	16.5	3.5
6.5	5.5	6.5	11.8	2.5
6.5	5.0	10.5	18.8	4.0

Spread the materials on top of the soil and/or grass in spring or early summer. The two sulfates will lower the pH in about two weeks; sulfur takes six to eight weeks. They will only make the first few inches of the ground more acidic and will not effect other flowering plants, shrubs or trees.

● Mosses I have grown do best on a compact, clay-type smooth soil surface. Poor ground is superior to a rich, fertile soil.

● Banks and steeper slopes are a problem because rain continually washes the spores away before they can germinate. Use railroad ties, logs or rocks to deflect water run-off in these areas until the moss has taken hold.

Moss can be transplanted, preferably in early spring when the weather is cool and the earth moist. When moving moss, take small clumps with a little soil to keep the plants from falling apart (one exception is fern moss, which can be rolled up without any soil and remains intact). Loosely scratch the ground where you will be planting and press the moss down firmly so there are no air spaces between the plants and soil. Be sure to keep the area moist for several weeks.

Another way to establish moss is to put a handful in a blender with one-half teaspoon of sugar and one can of beer. Spread this soupy mixture over bare ground or rocks. I have tried this twice, and it really works. You can substitute buttermilk for beer. You can also put bricks in a container of shallow water and cover the tops of the bricks with this mixture. Place in a cool, shady spot.

There is one important maintenance chore involved with beds or lawns of moss: remove all covering leaves in the fall. Moss plants will smother and die if the leaves remain. So, how do you rake off the leaves without disturbing the moss? It's difficult, but there are some easy solutions. One is to blow the leaves away with a leaf blower. Another is to rake them with a plastic rake when the ground is frozen. I've found the best method is to spread one-quarter-inch plastic mesh netting over the moss the end of August. When all the leaves have fallen, simply roll up the netting and put the leaves on your compost pile.

Ground Covers for Shade

Why struggle with lawn when there are scores of interesting plants that thrive in low light?

BY KEN DRUSE

*W*hen you think of ground covers for shade, you most likely picture the three familiar standbys: *Vinca minor* (vinca or periwinkle), *Pachysandra terminalis* (pachysandra or Japanese spurge) and *Hedera helix* (English ivy). They are good and reliable plants; but by no means is the selection limited to these. Even within their genera are options. There are well over one hundred varieties of English ivy — several of which are evergreen. One pachysandra has variegated foliage (*P. t.* 'Variegata') and new introductions are more compact and have lobed or serrated leaflets. There is even an American native species, *P. procumbens*, Allegheny spurge.

Finding a ground cover for a specific site has as much to do with the desired effect as with its covering potential and shade tolerance. Any plant that "covers" is a candidate — that is, if it spreads in some way — either by underground stems, stolons or runners, ever-expanding clumps or simply by growing wider and wider above the ground.

The big three all have flowers. Vinca has lovely violet flowers in spring, and there are varieties available with wine-red or white ones. Pachysandra has fuzzy flower spikes at the ends of the stems. Ivy blooms when it is mature: The flowers are insignificant, but the fruits, black beads in umbrellalike clusters, are quite ornamental. However, none of these is grown for its flowers; and truly, many of the best ground covers have flowers that are nothing to speak of.

The wild gingers are low foliage plants for shade. Most are slow to become generously established. The two most popular are the American deciduous native, *Asarum canadense*, with matte green leaves, and the usually evergreen

Clockwise from top left: *Hosta* 'Kabitan', *Asarum canadense*, *Hosta* 'Louisa' and *Pachysandra procumbens*, allegheny spurge.

European ginger, *A. europaeum*. *A virginicum* is a solid green form with shiny, heart-shaped leaves. *A. arifolium*, called *Hexastylis arifolia* in the South, has arrow-shaped leaves mottled with silver. Among the most beautiful is *A. shuttleworthii* with exquisite silver-flecked or veined green leaves, but it is not as winter hardy as *A. canadense* or *A. europaeum*. You would have to crawl on the ground to see the flowering structures of these plants — reddish brown, upside-down urns about a half inch long that nearly touch the soil.

Plants whose foliage resembles the gingers include the natives *Galax urceolata* and *Shortia galacifolia*. Although considered here for their foliage, they are prized for their lovely flowers in woodland gardens. The former has white stars on a spike thrust above the foliage; the latter, white or pink fringed bells.

Pulmonarias, the lungworts (the "wort" refers to a plant once thought to possess medicinal value), have spectacular fuzzy green leaves that are often speckled, striped or splashed with silver. They also have long-lasting flowers — blue, pink, red or white. There are other ground covers with beautiful flowers, such as *Phlox stolonifera*, creeping phlox, with ten-inch-tall pink, white or lavender flower stalks that completely hide the three-inch-high foliage in spring. *P. divaricata* will colonize an area in time, and has some of the most beautiful flowers of the spring — most often blue, but there are white-flowered varieties and deep lavender with a red eye.

For temporary color and cover, impatiens can't be surpassed. If these annuals get too tall, cut them back — even to leafless stems — and they'll come back in short order. But beyond this ubiquitous shade-appreciating annual, there are many flower-border perennials to use as ground covers. For example, in partial shade, try *Astilbe chinensis pumila* with orchid-lavender flowers. *A.* 'Sprite' has handsome pink flowers and wonderful ferny foliage. Both are short in stature.

Some of the lowest covers include the beautiful flowering ajugas, which are desirable for their leaf colors and spring flowers on spikes that shoot up above the foliage. *Ajuga reptans* 'Burgundy Glow' has gray-green leaves suffused with magenta and wine-purple and edged in white. *A.* 'Metallica' is one of the most common and vigorous varieties and will run-over other selections. It has very pretty leaves much like beet green. *A.* 'Silver Beauty' has green and white foliage and like the others is a more moderate spreader than 'Metallica'. *A.* 'Argentea' actually does have silvery foliage. All of these have spiky blue flowers in spring. *Lamium*

Clockwise from top left: *Epimedium grandiflorum, Lamium maculatum, Vinca minor* and *Epimedium pinnatum.*

maculatum, the dead nettles, come in several varieties. *L.m.* 'Beacon Silver' has silvery leaves with green margins and deep pink flowers. The cultivar 'White Nancy' has beautiful white flowers.

Other flowering ground covers include the Lily-of-the-valley (*Convallaria majalis*), whose familiar fragrant bells are borne around Father's Day. Violets can be considered either desirable covers or the lawn-lover's nemesis, but some of the more unusual kinds might have the makings of a collection. Look for creeping *Viola labradorica* with maroon foliage, and *V. cucullata* 'Freckles' with speckled flowers, for two of the more interesting and easy-to-grow kinds. If you have a bit of sun, comfrey (*Symphytum grandiflorum*) with tons of cream-colored flowers, is astonishing.

Green and gold (*Chrysogonum virginianum*) is a native ground cover that looks a bit like a trailing *Rudbeckia*. It will bloom through the season in dappled shade, and can grow with average to dry soil moisture. *Lysimachia nummularia* (moneywort or creeping jenny) has tiny, green, coin-shaped leaves and lovely yellow flowers held close to the low, trailing stems. It likes moist spots. There is a wonderful variety with chartreuse leaves (*L.n.* 'Aurea', but it is not as vigorous as the species, and needs more sun).

Galium odoratum is the common sweet woodruff — once used to flavor May wine. It has delicate whorls of light green leaves on trailing stems, and is covered with snowy white flowers in mid to late spring. It makes an airy cover under open shrubs such as deciduous azaleas. Foam flower, *Tiarella cordifolia*, is known for its fuzzy white or pink floral spikes — rightly so, but don't overlook the handsome maplelike foliage. As a colony of these native plants ages and increases in size, it will prove a dense cover. With gentle help from you, dividing and replanting every spring, the process can be accelerated. Heucheras can be used similarly — some species and varieties want more sun than others. Although the heucheras flower (they are commonly called coral bells for the little bell-like flowers on tall wiry stems), some have simple, pale blooms that are barely noticeable for the color and size of the leaves. Look for varieties of *H. americana* and *H. villosa* for naturalizing.

When there is competition from tree roots — the dreaded dry shade — you'll have to experiment. It isn't a good idea to pile soil on top of tree roots. That

Clockwise from top left: bronze-edged epimedium, *Asarum shuttleworthii*, Ajuga 'Burgundy Glow' and a variegated liriope.

could kill the trees by cutting off moisture and air. In the worst-case scenarios — maple or beech trees — consider planting in containers raised above the ground on bricks. Impatiens or coleus can fill wooden tubs, or you might build a permanent stand for summering house plants there. In light shade, perhaps between the exposed roots of trees and among stones of a somewhat shady rock garden, try *Iris cristata*, the crested iris. This tiny rhizomatous plant has lavender or white flowers. Look also for new cultivars with flowers in a range of shades from light to deep purple.

In the dry shade beneath deeply rooted trees you might also try epimediums, the barrenworts. These plants like some sun for good flowering, but seem to tolerate root competition if the soil is rich in humus. Flowers come in nearly every color but true blue. *E.* x *youngianum* 'Niveum' is a low-growing hybrid with spectacular snow-white flowers. *E. grandiflorum* has large flowers that face the ground and have petals the color of grape lifesaver candy with pale centers.

Liriope species, sometimes called lilyturf, are grown for their strappy, semievergreen, grassy leaves. There are several variegated forms. And all have hyacinthlike flowers, most often violet, sometimes white. They often produce attractive black berries. I think this is a difficult plant to blend well in the garden — especially the variegated ones, which can be rather bright yellow and green. But they can be effective if used to edge a long sidewalk in the shade of the house, or when the strappy texture is contrasted with dissimilar foliage such as hosta leaves.

Hostas are, of course, about the best known herbaceous perennials for shade, and any of them can be used as ground cover. Kinds that "fill in" rather than just form round clumps are especially useful. These spreaders include *Hosta* 'Allan P. McConnell', *H. gracillima* 'Variegated', 'Ground Master', 'Kabitan', 'Gold Standard' and 'Louisa'. You can also collect some of the golden-leafed varieties such as 'Golden Scepter' or 'Wogon Gold', so that you can "light up" the shade with a colorful ground-covering plant. All of these bloom, too.

Most of the plants mentioned above are recommended for those parts of the country that receive at least 40 inches of rain a year and in which forest is the dominant native plant community. Gardeners in other regions can also perk up the shade using easy-care ground covers appropriate for their areas.

KEN DRUSE *is the author of* The Natural Garden *(1989)* The Natural Shade Garden *(1992) and the forthcoming* The Natural Habitat Garden *(1994), all published by Clarkson N. Potter. He gardens in New York City.*

Sedge Lawns

The new American lawn

BY JOHN GREENLEE

ew breakthroughs in the history of turf have been as significant as the arrival of a whole new kind of lawn — the sedge lawn. Sedges are close botanical cousins of the grasses and look a lot like them. Properly selected and planted, sedges can function as a traditional lawn and require little or no mowing, fertilizing or chemicals. Some require less water than many conventional turf grasses. Others tolerate wet, moist areas, and many thrive in shade. What's more, sedge lawns restore something of the character of the native sods that existed before agriculture and development transformed the American landscape.

A meadow of Pennsylvania sedge, *Carex pennsylvanica*. Sedges are best grown in the regions in which they are native.

The conventional lawn, which, believe it or not, now covers more than 50,000 square miles across the continent, consists of grasses from Africa, Asia, Europe and other places. The native sods composed of sedges and grasses have largely been replaced by these foreign, high-maintenance species. It has reached a point that today, very little remains of the native sods. Perhaps the new American lawn is the original sod just waiting to be rediscovered.

Part of the attraction of the genus *Carex*, into which sedges fall, is its tremendous variety and adaptability. There are more than 2,000 species of *Carex*, and they are found in a wide range of habitats in nature. They vary from miniatures with foliage only one to two inches high, to specimens growing to three or four feet. Some creep, some clump, some do a little of both. They can be found in sun or shade, in wet soils or heavy clay, from coastal dunes to alpine scree. In almost every ecosystem, there is at least one *Carex*. In most there are many, and at least one candidate with good lawnlike qualities.

Sedge meadow meets informal flower border in southern California.

Five sedges that have shown excellent promise as substitutes for traditional lawn grasses are *Carex texensis*, the catlin sedge, *Carex planostachys*, the cedar sedge, *Carex pennsylvanica* var. *gracilifolia* and other varieties of Pennsylvania sedge, *Carex pansa*, the California meadow sedge, and *Carex praegracilis* 'Laguna Mountain', a selection of the western meadow sedge.

These five native sedges have been selected for their compact growth, good green color and mostly evergreen foliage. They also tolerate varying degrees of shade and competition from tree roots.

Below are descriptions of the five *Carex* species. They are best grown in the regions in which they are native and to which they are adapted. Many more sedges are being collected and identified in the wild, and hybridization also offers enormous possibilities.

CAREX TEXENSIS

(FORMERLY CAREX RETROFLEXA)

Catlin Sedge

This native Southwestern sedge has naturalized in parts of California. It mingles in nature with other sedges and it or close relatives are adapted to a wide range of the southern United States with proven hardiness to USDA zone 7. It makes a fine lawn or meadow, both mowed and unmowed. It tolerates a close mowing and grows 3" to 4" unmowed. It will grow from seed or plugs, though seed may be hard to come by. Plant plugs 4" to 8" on center. Mowing will increase sod formation. The catlin sedge is clumping by nature, so plant plugs close together for lawns. This sedge makes a fine lawn for southern California. It thrives in sun or shade and looks best with regular water.

JOHN GREENLEE

Catlin sedge comes right up to and mingles with the flowering border. It can be mowed or left unmowed.

CAREX PLANOSTACHYS

Cedar Sedge

This Texas native is another fine lawnlike sedge. It is drought and moisture tolerant with dark green foliage 4" to 6" high. It is slowly creeping, almost clump forming. It does equally well in sun or shade, and is hardy to USDA zone 6 and possibly lower. Plant from plugs; it is largely untested from seed. Plant plugs 6" to 8" on center. It looks best with regular water but will tolerate periods of summer drought.

CAREX PENNSYLVANICA

Pennsylvania Sedge

The Pennsylvania sedge has a wide distribution throughout the eastern United States. Extremely adaptable and widely variable in nature, this sedge and its varieties are some of the most promising lawn substitutes. Some are creeping, others form dense mats or tufts or form clumps. They vary from 1" to 2" miniatures to 8" to 10" clones. A particularly fine cultivar, *C. pennsylvanica* var. *gracilifolia* 'Hilltop', is a selection from Towson, Maryland. Its extremely graceful, dark green foliage holds its color throughout the winter. It makes a durable lawn for sun or shade and is tolerant of close mowing and heavy traffic. The hilltop sedge grows 2" to 4" high unmowed. Early indications are that this sedge will do fine in the Pacific Northwest as well. Many more forms of this species are certain to come. Plant *Carex pennsylvanica* from plugs 6" to 8" on center.

JOHN GREENLEE

A mixed sedge lawn, predominanthly catlin sedge, with annual grasses in Pomona, California.

CAREX PANSA

California Meadow Sedge

Native from California to Washington, this sedge makes an excellent lawn, growing 4" to 6" high unmowed with a slowly creeping, non-invasive habit. Though somewhat slow in heavy soils, it will cover quickly in well drained, sandy soils. It tolerates heavy clay but prefers good drainage and full sun. It also tolerates medium shade with ease. Plant plugs 6" to 12" on center. This is a good choice for heavy traffic areas as the sod can repair itself.

CAREX PRAEGRACILIS

Western Meadow Sedge

This native western sedge and its varieties are found throughout western North America. 'Laguna Mountain', a particularly fine variety collected near Laguna Mountain in San Diego County, has been selected for its dark green color and compact growth. Its slowly creeping habit makes it a fine choice for lawns in sun or shade. Tolerant of heavy soils and heavy traffic, this sedge has so far proven one of the best lawn sedges for Western gardens. It has shown good drought tolerance and should become an important part of Western horticulture in the years to come. Plant plugs 6" to 12" on center.

SOURCES

KURT BLUEMEL, INC.

2740 Greene Lane

Baldwin, MD 21013

410-557-7229

Catalog, $3

GREENLEE NURSERY

301 E. Franklin Avenue

Pomona, CA 91766

714-629-9045

Catalog $5

PRAIRIE NURSERY

P.O.Box 306

Westfield, WI 53964

1-800-GRO-WILD

Catalog, $3

JOHN GREENLEE *established Greenlee Nursery in 1985. He is the author of* An Encyclopedia of Ornamental Grasses *(Rodale, 1992).*

Prairie

An all-American lawn alternative

BY NEIL DIBOLL

*A*re you tired of spending valuable free time mowing and maintaining your lawn? Would you like to help preserve part of our natural heritage and restore valuable habitat in your backyard? Then you should seriously consider converting your lawn into a native prairie.

Interest in using native prairie grasses and wildflowers in the landscape has been growing at a rapid rate. These include a wide selection of showy flowers and ornamental grasses that require a minimum of maintenance. What's more, there is little or no need to use chemicals in the prairie landscape. Once established, prairies require no fertilizing, no watering, no spraying, little weeding and only annual mowing. There are prairie plants for dry soils, regular soils and moist soils. Prairie flowers provide a succession of bloom from spring into fall, and the late-season color of the grasses provides interest well into the winter. Butterflies and hummingbirds are attracted to the flowers, and songbirds utilize the ripening seeds in autumn. The overall effect is a dynamic, ever-changing landscape that reflects the rhythm of the seasons, year after year.

The first prairie plantings were done by ecologists whose primary interest was to preserve these plants from impending extirpation. Only 150 years ago, vast grasslands stretched as far as the eye could see, blanketing much of America's heartland with an ocean of colors and textures. Today, prairie is one of the rarest plant associations on the continent. The soil that the deep-rooted prairie grasses and flowers had created over the centuries was so fertile that it was systematically converted into cropland, leaving only a few small fragments in the odd corners where the plow did not reach. In a matter of decades, corn and wheat had replaced a complex and unique plant community. The prairie was almost completely destroyed before it could be studied and fully appreciated.

Over the centuries, the native prairie plants have evolved to survive the extreme conditions of the Upper Midwest — drought, searing summer heat, severe winters and the ravages of grazing by vast herds of bison and elk. In response, they have developed root systems double or triple the size of their above-ground growth. These large below-ground reserves of energy allow the plants to survive unfavorable conditions and recover from damage rapidly. The prairie grasses produce a thick mat of finely divided roots in the upper three to four feet of the soil, with some extending as far as nine feet deep. In order to compete with the grasses, many of the prairie flowers have root systems that extend far below those of the grasses, up to 15 feet and more in some cases. Others have enlarged underground storage organs such as bulbs, corms and rhizomes that allow them to endure periods of severe stress.

In addition to sharing the soil environment, prairie plants subdivide the growing season among themselves. Some experience peak activity in spring, some in summer and others in early fall. The average height of the plants in flower also increases as the season progresses, with taller flowers coming up over the earlier-blooming, shorter members of the community. Many of the spring-blooming prairie flowers go dormant or near-dormant by midsummer, making way for the coneflowers, blazingstars, sunflowers and myriad of other summer bloomers. Asters, goldenrods and gentians produce the season's floral finale. Then, with the first frost, the various grasses don their winter plumage of bronze-reds and golden straw colors. In this way many different plants can occupy a given area, with each contributing to the successive waves of color that wash across the prairie landscape.

Seeds or Plants?

When you think of a prairie, the image of a seemingly endless meadow rolling toward the horizon probably comes to mind. However, prairie plants can be used in a variety of situations, from gardens a few square feet in size to plantings of many hundred acres. Almost all of the prairie plants can be used effectively in borders, either mixed with other perennials or as a "pure prairie" garden. More and more gardeners are creating small meadows of one acre or less, often to replace high-maintenance lawn. More and more people are discovering that their prairie meadow offers them a far more exciting landscape than their lawn, and at a fraction of the long-term cost. There are prairie flowers for dry soils and moist soils, which often present landscaping dilemmas for less durable, traditional garden plants. Many of the shorter species are excellent candidates for rock gardens. A combination of the showier flowers makes a very effective butterfly garden, and in areas with appropriate surrounding habitat, they can also bring in hummingbirds. A large number of the flowers and grasses provide both nutritious seeds and protective cover for songbirds. Even a small planting of only a few hundred square feet can become a focal point for many of these delightful garden visitors.

Prairie dropseed, *Sporobolus heterolepsis*, in autumn.

You can establish a prairie meadow using plants or seeds, or both. Small areas of a thousand square feet or less can be easily installed using plants. A general rule of thumb is to give each plant one square foot of space, although some require less and others more. With transplants, you can control the relationship of each plant to the others and create various combinations and effects. Most transplants will bloom the year they are installed, but a few very long-lived varieties may require two years or more to reach maturity. It's not unusual for many of these plants to live for 25 years or more. Many reproduce vegetatively, producing offshoots that live on after the original portion of the plant has died.

Seeding is somewhat trickier and inevitably results in a more random effect.

It is by far the most cost-effective method for planting large areas, but requires longer for the plants to reach maturity. Many prairie seeds grow readily on an open seedbed, while some require very specific conditions for germination and growth. This is why plants and seed are sometimes used in conjunction with each another. First the seeds are planted. Then transplants of the more difficult-to-grow species are installed, either directly following seeding or one or two years later, after the seeded area has become established.

Preparing the Site

Whether you're using seeds or plants, make sure that the area to be planted is free of grass, weeds, brush or any other competing vegetation. Most native plants are long lived, but slow growing. Weeds grow rapidly and can outcompete and stunt your wildflowers and grasses in the early going. Gaining control of the planting zone is your first priority.

There are a number of ways to prepare your site. On small areas, sod can be dug out, or removed using a sod-cutter. Or you can smother the undesirable plants using black plastic, old pieces of plywood or any other material that cuts off sunlight to the plants below. Leave the soil covered for two to three months during the growing season to kill the plants there. If brush or small trees are present, you'll need to mow them back to the ground before smothering.

The simplest way to prepare a large area in a short time is to use a low-toxicity glyphosate herbicide, such as Roundup. Spray the area when the plants are actively growing and well developed. Lawns can be killed with a single spraying in fall or spring. Because not all plants will be affected by the herbicide at any given time of the year, weedy fields may require repeated spraying, two or three times, throughout the growing season.

If you prefer not to use herbicides, you can work up the area by repeated tilling. Lawns can usually be prepared for planting with only two good tillings. Beware of weedy fields or lawns with weedy grasses in them! Simply plowing or tilling will not do the job. Rhizomatous perennial weeds are particularly difficult to kill, because they can resprout from a small section of root. You may have to till the area all summer long, every two to three weeks in order to kill difficult weeds such as quackgrass, Canada goldenrod, Canada thistle and Johnsongrass. If your site is sloping or rolling, tilling may not be an option, as it may encourage erosion. Clay, loamy and silty soils tend to be more subject to erosion than sandy soils. Glyphosate herbicide may be the best option for erodible soils on sloping sites.

Small areas of a few thousand square feet can be successfully seeded by hand

A swallowtail perches on a purple coneflower, *Echinacea purpurea.*

broadcasting seed and raking it into the soil, then rolling the area to assure firm seed-to-soil contact. The procedure is very similar to planting lawn grass. However, much less prairie seed is required per area compared to lawn grass, so the prairie seeds must be mixed with sawdust, vermiculite or peat moss to dilute them to ensure good coverage.

To increase germination, water for the first two months after planting. Water only in the morning to prevent fungal disease problems that can occur with night watering. After two months, your seedlings should have good root systems and will only need to be watered during prolonged dry spells during the first summer.

The first year after seeding a prairie planting, many people are exasperated when all they see is a field of weeds! But there's no reason to despair, as prairie denizens concentrate first on building their tremendous root systems. In the first year, many of the seedlings may only grow to one or two inches in height, yet have roots well over a foot long. By the second year, biennials such as black-eyed Susan will make their appearance, and a few of the faster-growing perennial flowers and grasses may bloom. In the third year, many different flowers will reach maturity and weeds should become less abundant as the native vegetation squeezes them out. By the fourth and fifth years, with a small amount of management (burning, or mowing and raking in mid-spring), the prairie plants should be in full control and well on their way to forming a long-term, self-sustaining community. As with any investment, patience is required. Five years is not long to wait for a landscape that will last a lifetime.

Dry, Medium or Moist Soils

There are prairie plants for almost any type of soil, be it dry, medium or moist. The shorter varieties tend to occur on dry, sandy or gravelly soils, as these soils generally possess lower levels of moisture and nutrients and cannot support the needs of most larger plants. Heights range from a few inches up to three or four feet tall. Some of the deeper-rooted taller flowers and grasses can also grow on dry soils, but the shorter ones tend to predominate and many are restricted to this environment. Many spring and fall-blooming species are common to dry prairies, because higher moisture levels and lower temperatures provide better growing conditions during these seasons. Soil moisture often becomes limiting during the heat of summer on dry soils, and only those plants with very deep roots or special adaptations can remain active. Nevertheless, a good selection of summer-blooming flowers is available for dry soils. Indeed, low-nutrient dry soils are often the easiest to successfully seed to native flowers and grasses because they do not provide a hospitable environment for large weeds that can overtop the young seedlings and retard their growth. Fertile soils, on the other hand, are often subject to heavy weed growth and usually require mowing to a height of six inches once or twice in the first year to allow light to reach the prairie seedlings below.

The widest selection of prairie flowers grows on well drained medium or "mesic" soils, such as sandy loams, silt loams and clay loams. Mesic soils were home to the tallgrass prairie. These soils have enough water- and nutrient-holding capacity to support most of the taller flowers, and many of the shorter varieties will grow well on these sites as well. Most range in height from two to five feet, with a few that will reach six feet or more. Because mesic soils can supply good levels of

Nodding pink onion, *Allium cernuum*, is a good choice for soils that aren't too dry or too moist.

moisture well into the growing season, blooming activity peaks during the long hot days of summer. This explosion of color in June, July and August is the hallmark of the mesic prairie. When most of the wildflower gardener's woodland flowers have finished blooming and the lawn is threatening to call it quits without its daily dose from the sprinkler, there stand the prairie flowers in their greatest glory!

The zone of transition between wetlands and the upland prairie is the natural habitat of the moist prairie. Here are found some of the grandest and most robust of all our native herbaceous perennials, along with some of the showiest — queen of the prairie, cardinal flower, turk's cap lily, prairie blazingstar, New England aster and many other beauties. Most members of the wet prairie community grow to four or five feet, but a few can reach as high as eight to ten feet.

Because wet soils are slow to warm up in spring, most floral activity occurs from mid-summer into early autumn. Many of these plants are capable of withstanding extended periods of flooding when dormant (from late fall until early spring), and are ideal for landscaping along pond edges and streambanks. However, most of them require an unsaturated, aerated zone in the upper soil during the growing season, and should not be planted in areas with standing water all year long. They will also thrive in a rich garden soil that is supplied with sufficient moisture, and some are capable of growing on mesic soils as well.

With this diversity of spectacular native plants suitable for a variety of applications, it's clear why prairie plants are growing ever more popular. Although little now remains of these once-vast flower gardens, the plants that composed them live on. Today, we can incorporate these beautiful flowers and grasses into our own landscapes and enjoy their constantly changing parade of color year after year. And with all the time saved on maintenance, that leaves more time for enjoyment!

NEIL DIBOLL *is President of Prairie Nursery in Westfield, Wisconsin.*

PAMELA HARPER

Joe Pye weed, *Eupatorium maculatum*, thrives in moist soils.

Prairie Plants

Leadplant (*Amorpha canescens*)

Pasque flower (*Anemone patens*)

Sky blue aster (*Aster azureus*)

Heath aster (*Aster ericoides*)

Smooth aster (*Aster laevis*)

Silky aster (*Aster sericeus*)

White aster (*Aster ptarmicoides*)

Butterflyweed (Asclepias tuberosa)

Canada milk vetch (*Astragalus canadensis*)

Harebell (*Campanula rotundifolia*)

Lance-leaf coreopsis (*Coreopsis lanceolata*)

Pale purple coneflower (*Echinacea pallida*)

Flowering spurge (*Euphorbia corollata*)

Downy sunflower (*Helianthus mollis*)

Western sunflower (*Helianthus occidentalis*)

Alum root (*Heuchera richardsonii*)

Rough blazingstar (*Liatris aspera*)

Dwarf blazingstar (*Liatris cylindracea*)

Dotted blazingstar (*Liatris punctata*)

Hairy puccoon (*Lithospermum carolinense*)

Lupine (*Lupinus perennis*)

Bergamot (*Monarda fistulosa*)

Dotted Mint (*Monarda punctata*)

Beardtongue (*Penstemon grandiflorus*)

Purple prairie clover (*Dalea purpurea*)

Prairie buttercup (*Ranunculus rhomboideus*)

Black-eyed Susan (*Rudbeckia hirta*)

Stiff goldenrod (*Solidago rigida*)

Showy goldenrod (*Solidago speciosa*)

Spiderwort (*Tradescantia ohiensis*)

Hoary Vervain (*Verbena stricta*)

Big bluestem (*Andropogon gerardii*)

Little bluestem (*Schizachyrium scoparium*)

Sideoats grama (*Bouteloua curtipendula*)

Canada wild rye (*Elymus canadensis*)

Junegrass (*Koeleria cristata*)

Switchgrass (*Panicum virgatum*)

Indiangrass (*Sorghastrum nutans*)

Prairie dropseed (*Sporobolus heterolepsis*)

Prairie smoke (*Geum triflorum*)

Nodding pink onion (*Allium cernuum*)

Butterflyweed (*Asclepias tuberosa*)

Sky blue aster (*Aster azureus*)

Smooth aster (*Aster laevis*)

White false indigo (*Baptisia lactea*)

Cream false indigo (*Baptisia leucophaea*)

New Jersey tea (*Ceanothus americanus*)

Shootingstar (*Dodecatheon meadia*)

Pale purple coneflower (*Echinacea pallida*)

New England aster *(Aster novae-angliae)*

Purple coneflower (*Echinacea purpurea*)

Blue false indigo *(Baptisia australis)*

Rattlesnake master (*Eryngium yuccifolium*)

Ox-eye sunflower (*Heliopsis helianthoides*)

Prairie blazingstar (*Liatris pycnostachya*)

Rocky Mountain blazingstar (*Liatris ligulistylis*)

Wild quinine (*Parthenium integrifolium*)

Smooth penstemon (*Penstemon digitalis*)

White prairie clover (*Dalea candida*)

Heartleaf golden Alexanders *(Zizia aptera)*

Bergamot *(Monarda fistulosa)*

Great Solomon's seal (*Polygonatum biflorum*)

Yellow coneflower (*Ratibida pinnata*)

Sweet black-eyed Susan (*Rudbeckia subtomentosa*)

Compassplant (*Silphium laciniatum*)

Prairie dock (*Silphium terebinthinaceum*)

Stiff goldenrod (*Solidago rigida*)

Spiderwort (*Tradescantia ohiensis*)

Culver's root (*Veronicastrum virginicum*)

Big bluestem (*Andropogon gerardii*)

Black-eyed Susan *(Rudbeckia hirta)*

Little bluestem (*Schizachyrium scoparium*)

Canada wild rye (*Elymus canadensis*)

Switchgrass (*Panicum virgatum*)

Indiangrass (*Sorghastrum nutans*)

Prairie dropseed (*Sporobolus heterolepsis*)

Red milkweed (*Asclepias incarnata*)

New England aster (*Aster novae-angliae*)

White false indigo (*Baptisia lactea*)

Turtlehead (*Chelone glabra*)

Tall coreopsis (*Coreopsis tripteris*)

Joe Pye weed (*Eupatorium maculatum*)

Queen of the prairie (*Filipendula rubra*)

Bottle gentian (*Gentiana andrewsii*)

Great blue lobelia *(Lobelia siphilitica)*

Cardinal flower *(Lobelia cardinalis)*

Glade mallow (*Napaea dioica*)

False dragonhead (*Physostegia virginiana*)

Yellow coneflower (*Ratibida pinnata*)

Green headed coneflower (*Rudbeckia laciniata*)

Sweet black-eyed Susan (*Rudbeckia subtomentosa*)

Cupplant (*Silphium perfoliatum*)

Blue vervain (*Verbena hastata*)

Ironweed (*Vernonia fasciculata*)

Culver's root (*Veronicastrum virginicum*)

Golden alexanders (*Zizia aurea*)

Big bluestem (*Andropogon gerardii*)

Bluejoint grass (*Calamagrostis canadensis*)

Prairie cordgrass (*Spartina pectinata*)

Porcupine sedge (*Carex hystericina*)

Fox sedge (*Carex vulpinoidea*)

Sneezeweed *(Helenium autumnale)*

Wild iris (*Iris shrevei*)

Dense blazingstar (*Liatris spicata*)

Turk's cap lily (*Lilium superbum*)

These plants and many more are available from Prairie Nursery. For a 2-year subscription to their 48-page color catalog, send $3 to Prairie Nursery, P.O. Box 306, Westfield, WI 53964 or call 1-800-GRO-WILD.

Index

Acid soil, 62, 66
Actinomycetes, 23, 26
Aerating, 24-25
Ageratum, wild (*Eupatorium coelestinum*), 59
Ajuga reptans, 70, 72
Allegheny spurge (*Pachysandra procumbens*) 68, 69
Alum root (*Heuchera richardsonii*), 89
Asters, 89, 90, 92
Astilbe chinensis pumila, 70
Avens (*Geum canadense*), 56, 57

Bahiagrass
    mowing, 31
    by region, 28
Barrenwort. See Epimediums
Beardtongue (*Penstemon grandiflorus*), 89
Bentgrass, 33
    mowing, 31
    by region, 29
Bergamot (*Monarda fistulosa*), 89
Bermudagrass
    mowing, 31
    by region, 28, 29
Black-eyed Susans (*Rudbeckia*), 16, 58, 86, 89, 91, 92
Blazing stars (*Liatris*), 89, 90, 92
Bluejoint grass, 92
Bluestems
    Andropogon gerardii (big), 89, 91, 92
    Schizachyrium scoparium (little), 89, 91
Bluets (*Hedyotis caerulea*), 65
Buffalograss

advantages of, 46-48
    mowing, 31
    by region, 28, 29, 47, 49
    requirements of, 48-49
Butterflyweed (*Asclepias tuberosa*), 16, 89, 90

Canada lily (*Lilium canadensis*), 16
Canada milk vetch (*Astragalus canadensis*), 89
Canada wild rye (*Elymus canadensis*), 89, 91
Cardinal flower (*Lobelia cardinalis*), 92
Carolina jessamine (*Gelsemium sempervirens*), 56
Centipedegrass
    mowing, 31
    by region, 28
Christmas fern (*Polystichum acrostichoides*), 65
Columbine (*Aquilegia canadensis*), 56
Comfrey (*Symphytum grandiflorum*), 73
Compassplant (*Silphium laciniatum*), 91
Compost, 23, 26, 39
Coneflowers
    Echinacea, 85, 89, 90
    Ratibida pinnata (yellow), 91, 92
    Rudbeckia laciniata (green headed), 92
Coral bells (*Heuchera*), 73
Coral honeysuckle (*Lonicera sempervirens*), 56
Coreopsis
    lanceolata (lanceleaf), 58, 89
    tripteris (tall), 92

Cottonseed meal, 21-22
Crabgrass, 11, 22
Creeping jenny (*Lysimachia nummularia*), 73
Crow poison (*Nothoscordum bivalve*), 56
Culver's root (*Veronicastrum virginicum*), 91, 92
Cupplant (*Silphium perfoliatum*), 92

Dandelions, 22-23
Dotted mint (*Monarda punctata*), 89
Drainage problems, 39

Elm (*Ulmus americanus*), 59
Endophytes, 33
English ivy (*Hedera helix*), 69
Epimediums, 71, 72, 74
Eve's necklace (*Sophora affinis*), 55

False dragonhead (*Physostegia virginiana*), 92
False indigo (*Baptisia*), 90, 92
Fertilizers
    chemical, 21
    maintenance schedule, 30
    natural, 11, 21-22, 26
    nitrogen content, 30
    phosphorus content, 40-41
Fescues, 20
    fine, 22, 28, 29, 31, 32, 36
    improved varieties, 35-36
    insect-resistant, 33
    invasive, 33
    mowing, 22, 31
    by region, 28, 29
    tall, 28, 29, 31, 32, 33, 35
Fields and meadows
    annual mowing, 14

mowed perimeter, 10
natural seeding, 16
nesting birds in, 14, 16
poison ivy control, 16-17
See also Prairie
Fish emulsion, 22
Flowering spurge (*Euphorbia corollata*), 89
Foamflower (*Tiarella cordifolia*), 64, 65, 73

Galax urceolata, 70
Gentiana
andrewsii (bottle), 92
crinita (fringed), 16
Gingers, wild (*Asarum*), 69-70
Glade mallow (*Napaea dioica*), 92
Golden alexanders (*Zizia aurea*), 92
Goldenrod (*Solidago*), 89, 91
Grading, 40
Grass(es)
disease resistant, 20
improved varieties, 32, 34-37
insect-resistant, 33
invasive, 33
by region, 28-29
zones of United States, 29
See also Lawn, Seeding, names of grasses
Grass clippings, 11, 26
Great Solomon's seal (*Polygonatum biflorum*), 91
Green and gold (*Chrysogonum virginianum*), 73
Greeneyes (*Berlandiera texana*), 56, 57, 58, 59
Ground covers, 27
with moss, 65
native plants, 55-56
for shade, 69-74

Hairy puccoon (*Lithospermum carolinense*), 89
Harebell (*Campanula rotundifolia*), 89
Herbicides, 17, 38, 84
Horseherb (*Calyptocarpus*

vialis), 55
Hosta, 68, 74
Hydrangea arborescens, 57

Impatiens, 70
Indiangrass, 89
Insecticidal soap, 23
Insects
grasses resistant to, 33
natural control of, 23
Iris
Louisiana, 57
wild, 92
Ironweed (*Veronicastrum virginicum*), 92
Ivy, English (*Hedera helix*), 69

Japanese spurge (*Pachysandra terminalis*), 65, 69
Jessamine, Carolina (*Gelsemium sempervirens*), 56
Joe Pye weed (*Eupatorium maculatum*), 88, 92
Junegrass, 89

Kentucky bluegrass, 32
improved varieties, 37
invasive, 33
mowing, 22, 31
by region, 28, 29

Lamium maculatum, 70, 71, 73
Lawn
buffalograss, 46-49
conventional, 9-10, 51-52, 76
defense of, 19
purposeful, 10
renovation of, 38-43
sod removal methods, 38, 62, 84
See also Grass(es); Lawn, chemical-free; Seeding
Lawn, chemical-free, 18-27
aerating, 24-25
disease control, 23, 26
fertilizers, 11, 21-22, 26
insect control, 23, 33
monitoring, 27
mowing, 11, 22-23, 26
overseeding, 25-26

topdressing, 23, 25
weeding, 22-23
Lawn alternatives, 27
moss, 61-67
native plants, 53-59
sedges, 75-79
See also Fields and meadows; Ground covers; Prairie
Leadplant (*Amorpha canescens*), 89
Lily-of-the-valley (*Convallaria majalis*), 73
Lilyturf (*Liriope*), 72, 74
Lobelia siphilitica, 92
Lungwort, 71
Lupine (*Lupinus perennis*), 89

Manure, 21, 22, 23, 26
Meadow rue (*Thalictrum dasycarpum*), 56
Mexican buckeye (*Ungnadia speciosa*), 55
Milk vetch, Canada (*Astragalus canadensis*), 89
Milkweed, red (*Asclepias incarnata*), 92
Milky spore, 23
Moneywort (*Lysimachia nummularia*), 73
Moss, 61-67
fern (*Thuidium delicatulum*), 63, 64
haircap (*Polytrichum commune*), 62, 64
Mowing
fields and meadows, 14
heights by species, 31
high, 11, 22, 26, 31
Mulch, lawn clippings, 11

Native plants
garden, 53-59
prairie, 89-92
New Jersey tea (*Ceanothus americanus*), 90
Nitrogen
in fertilizers, 30
natural sources of, 21-22
Nodding pink onion (*Allium*

cernuum), 87, 90

Oak (*Quercus*), native garden, 59
Obedient plant (*Physostegia virginiana*), 56, 59
Overseeding, 25-26
Ox-eye sunflower (*Heliopsis helianthoides*), 90

Pachysandra
    procumbens (Allegheny spurge), 68, 69
    terminalis (Japanese spurge), 65, 69
Partridgeberry (*Mitchella repens*), 65
Pasque flower (*Anemone patens*), 89
Peat humus, 23, 39
Pecan (*Carya illinoinensis*), 59
Penstemon, 91
Periwinkle, See *Vinca*
Pesticides, 6, 19-20, 27
pH, 40, 62
Phlox, 16
    divaricata, 70
    paniculata, 58
    pilosa, 57
    stolonifera (creeping), 64, 65, 70
Phosphorus, in fertilizers, 40-41
Poison ivy, 16-17
Prairie, 13, 81-82
    five-year establishment period, 86
    plants, 89-92
    seeding, 83-85
    site preparation, 84
    soil, 86-88
    transplanting, 83
    See also Fields and meadows
Prairie buttercup (*Ranunculus rhomboideus*), 89
Prairie clover (*Dalea*), 89, 91
Prairie dock (*Silphium terebinthinaceum*), 91
Prairie dropseed, 89, 91

Prairie smoke (*Geum triflorum*), 89

Queen of the Prairie (*Filipendula rubra*), 92
Rattlesnake master (*Eryngium yuccifolium*), 90
Rhizoids, 63
Rotenone, 23
Roundup, 17, 84
Ruellia, 55, 56-57, 59
Ryegrass, perennial, 20, 32
    improved varieties, 34
    insect-resistant, 33
    invasive, 33
    mowing, 22, 31
    by region, 28, 29

Sabadilla dust, 23
Sage (*Salvia*), 58
    roemeriana (cedar), 57
St. Augustinegrass, 53, 54
    mowing, 31
    by region, 28
Salvia, See Sage
Sea oats (*Chasmanthium latifolium*), 56
Seaweed, liquid, 23
Sedges (*Carex*)
    California meadow, 76, 79
    Catlin, 76, 77
    Cedar, 76, 77-78
    fox, 92
    lawn of, 75-77
    Pennsylvania, 76, 78
    porcupine, 92
    sources for, 79
    western meadow, 76, 79
Seeding, 41-43
    overseeding, 25-26
    prairie, 83-85
    rolling/raking, 42
    seed mix, 41-42
    spot seeding, 43
    unfertilized soil, 40
    watering, 42-43
Shootingstar (*Dodecatheon meadia*), 90
Shortia galacifolia, 65, 71
Sideoats grama, 89

Sneezeweed (*Helenium autumnale*), 92
Soil
    acid, 62, 66
    aerating, 24-25
    compaction, 24
    drainage, 39
    organic content, 39-40
    pH, 40, 62
    prairie, 86-88
Spiderwort (*Tradescantia*), 57, 59, 89, 91
Sunflower (*Helianthus*), 89
Sweet woodruff (*Galium odoratum*), 73
Switchgrass, 89

Topdressing, 23, 25
Trumpet vine (*Campsis radicans*), 58
Turk's cap (*Malvaviscus arboreus*), 56, 57, 58, 87
Turk's cap lily (*Lilium superbum*), 92
Turtlehead (*Chelone glabra*), 92

Vervain (*Verbena*), 89, 92
Viburnum rufidulum (rusty blackhaw), 55
Vinca minor, 65, 69, 71
Violets (*Viola*)
    cucullata, 73
    labradorica, 73
    missouriensis, 56

Watering
    buffalograss, 48
    native plants, 54
    prairie plants, 85
    in seeding, 42-43
Weeding tools, 22-23
Wild quinine (*Parthenium integrifolium*), 90

Zexmenia (*Wedelia hispida*), 57-58, 59
Zoysia
    mowing, 31
    by region, 28, 29

BBG Gardening Guides

American Cottage Gardening

Annuals: A Gardener's Guide

Bonsai: Special Techniques

Culinary Herbs

Dyes from Nature

The Environmental Gardener

Garden Photography

The Gardener's World of Bulbs

Gardening for Fragrance

Gardening in the Shade

Gardening with Wildflowers & Native Plants

Greenhouses & Garden Rooms

Herbs & Cooking

Herbs & Their Ornamental Uses

Hollies: A Gardener's Guide

Indoor Bonsai

Japanese Gardens

A New Look at Vegetables

Orchids for the Home & Greenhouse

Ornamental Grasses

Perennials: A Gardener's Guide

Pruning Techniques

Roses

Soils

The Town & City Gardener

Trees: A Gardener's Guide

Water Gardening

The Winter Garden